edward j, o'toole

ALBA HOUSE

the better part

■ Division of the Society of St. Paul ■ Staten Island, N.Y. 10314

NIHIL OBSTAT:
George W. Shea
Censor Librorum

IMPRIMATUR:
Thomas A. Boland, S.T.D.
Archbishop of Newark
June 24, 1969

Library of Congress Catalog Card Number: 76-99139

Designed, printed and bound in the U.S.A. by the Pauline Fathers and Brothers of the Society of St. Paul at Staten Island, New York as a part of their communications apostolate.

SBN: 8189-0158-6

TABLE OF CONTENTS

Matri et Mariae
Both of whom have chosen
the better part.

APPRECIATION

A man must be totally immersed in his world. He is part of that world, and part of it in a special, human, personal manner. Unlike the things which lack consciousness and self-consciousness, the man is reflectively contained in his world. It is never foreign to him; it is his *only* home; it is his God-given birthright. God is not apart from the world in any spatial dimension. In a strangely unfamiliar usage of metaphore, all of us — and all of creation — are *in* God. This is the DIVINE PRESENCE of which Christ spoke so well; "I am in the Father and the Father is in Me." It is a cosmic immersion.

The Christian notion of "Image" is a take off from DIVINE PRESENCE. How else could it be explained that we reflect God's creative Hand, were it not that we imaged Him? For all our proximity to Christ, we set Him so far from ourselves. This is an error. It is an error in any case, but, for the Christian, it is the basest kind of error. To be far from Christ is never to have really known Him; so His last recorded words have no meaning, "I am with you always."

The present work is an attempt at reconciling, from a logically poetic point-of-view, the seemingly paradoxical statements of the Gospel Message. We have based ourselves upon a fundamental principle: Christ could not, and in fact does not, contradict Himself. The contradiction comes not from Christ, but from our futile efforts to make His words logically "understandable."

To those who have shown me this truth I am deeply grateful. I wish to thank especially:

My Family — whose belief is part of the better part.

Vincent F. Affanoso, my dear friend, whose "believing" helps my own.

My Students at Seton Hall who may question their Faith but never, never doubt it.

Mrs. Ruth Dolan, my secretary in the Philosophy Office, whose only faults are, paradoxically speaking, virtues. This is a fact which those who know her will understand.

Laus Deo et Omnibus Aliis Gratias.

PREFACE

These remarks are addressed to the mature Christian person. When I say that someone is a Christian, I am pointing to the obvious fact that he gives total fiducial assent to the Message of Christ, in its purest form, as discovered in the New Testament Writings. Christ sets him off in terms of a religious denominational class. The basis for membership in this class is the exclusive role that Christ plays in his life. Hence, "Intelligent Christian" means for us the intellectually mature person who totally accepts Christ.

The Christian Message can be termed both simple and complex, but, logically speaking, these descriptions do not pertain to the Message with an identical logical denotation. We call the Message simple, because, basically, it can be accepted by everyone with a firm religious assent. This assent is an unqualified affirmation of all the articles in the Apostles' Creed. The simplicity of the Message is such that, in the words of Christ, it is founded upon the "Love of God" and "Love of Neighbor." Complexity has no place here. The child, the adult, the professional, the theologian, in varying degrees, accept the same basic plan for living. This is Christian simplicity.

The complexity of the Message is discovered in a totally different context. The Message itself is a connected sequence of revealed meanings, which, by the very fact that they are meanings, are neither resolvable nor reducible to a single intelligible note. Any meaning whatever is multi-dimensional, but specifically Christian meanings are so to an infinitely greater degree. To know such a meaning precisely as complex is to seek a personal insight.

For the Christian, and rightly so, Revelation has a definite connotation. It means the fact of God communicating with men about those truths which transcend human understanding and surpass, in their meaningfulness, the power of the human mind to discover for itself. The body of revealed truths is a unique deposit to which every Christian gives, on the authority of God-speaking-through-Christ, the fullest recognition and certitude possible in any act of human knowing. In this instance alone, "Belief" becomes a level of knowledge which surpasses the common level of "human faith." Belief becomes super-natural such that the help of God supplies for the deficiencies of natural awareness. "Grace" raises the human cognitive powers to a level of perception that cannot be explained properly except in a theological frame-of-reference.

On the other hand language, as the most human means of communication, is a construct of sounds, both oral and written, which makes possible, on the plateau of discourse, the transferral of meaning through spoken words. Language is a communication based upon logical categories and grammatical meanings. It is founded upon the dictionary values attached to traditional sounds in a given culture. Language is for speaking human thoughts.

Revelation in language does present a problem for us which we cannot dismiss in a cavalier fashion. No matter how we view it, Revelation deals with transcendent truths made known in a super-natural way. These truths, for the most part, are such that the human person, situated entirely on his own, could not discover them by himself. They are hidden, either as existential prime discoveries or as in-comprehensible facts, from the unaided human vision. The Christian term for such divine communications is "Mysteries." They are

meaningful truths but incomprehensible; they are humanly transfer-
able, but not in a disciplined logical form. Logical form follows the
sequence patterns of some inferential methodology. It is fully equipped
to handle the problems which language is able to present to it. Beyond
this limit language cannot go. Mystery, especially in the Christian
sense, *is* beyond this limit. Mystery transcends the categories of
meaning upon which language is dependent. It is the step beyond.

Language cannot handle, in an adequate manner, the communication of mysteries, for it was never geared to do so. The truths to which
we lend our total credence are beyond our powers to grasp completely.
In language-form, they become at times paradoxical; in logical patterns
based upon the consistency of the universal or the defined particular,
they appear, in certain cases, to be contradictory. However, in the
language of Faith, they are completely acceptable. The logic of Faith is
totally different from the logic of language. Faith is always a shared
experience, even on the level of ordinary human knowledge. Its
evidential basis is the authoritative word of someone else. On the
transcendent level of Revelation, the authoritative basis for personal
acceptance is the word of God Himself. Such a foundation begets the
greatest mental certitude, since, for the believer, it excludes all
possibility of error.

Communication, on this level, is open only to the totally involved
person. Like the poet, who must communicate a feeling or emotion,
which cannot be defined in language terms, Faith must seek some form
of expression which is not classed or typed or otherwise universal.
There is something mystical about Mystery; something not entirely
communicable; something hidden but poetically felt. The Christian
Mystery is never seen in a simple, single, mental grasp; it must be
experienced within the unification of a thoroughly Christian frame-of-
reference.

To examine a Mystery properly, it must be reflected upon, not in an effort to exhaust its intelligibility, but rather with a view to making its intelligibility, as far as this is possible, purposeful in our lives. Hence, we should always look for insights. We seek by reflective thought to become involved as a total person in the world of Christ's Mysteries. This involvement, since it is of the total person, will not be merely intellectual, but inspirational and emotional as well. In reflecting on the Mystery we need never look for something "new." We are not seeking collective information in the sense of a catechism-type content. We seek to be inspired.

Since such inspiration is personal, we should never attempt the impossible task of universalizing it. We keep it singular, individual, concretely personal, as an experience all our own. Personal inspiration cannot be properly communicated, but it can help us to communicate in other ways. The Christian Mysteries, so absorbed into our lives, will be a preparation for the continuing dialogue that the words of Christ and the Mysteries of Revelation constantly urge us to attempt.

I.
SUCH ARE OUR THOUGHTS

I would so like to dream a dream with you.
  Not in the ordinary sense of "dream"; but more realistically, a mutual
  conscious endeavor.
Technically, dreams are not the romantic illusions
  that literature marks off in a special manner. Rather, they refer, at least in
  our day, to those unconscious awarenesses that are either
    hideous or beautiful, but still
      Come to us as asleep.
  Images we cannot control with our thinking selves.
    Which are there, caused by
      We know not.
Such dreams are presumed to have meanings and I have no quarrel with this.
Perhaps they do. Perhaps, in some strange manner, our questioning will raise
them to
  Some conscious level such that they
      "Mean" something.
I do not mean dreams like this.
    I mean rather the dream of the Prophet or the Poet. I mean that dream
    we fashion when awake. I mean an inner fantasy, based on
    experience, which we conjur up at those moments in life when we are
    fully alive, vital, and human —
As when we see a sunset,
    And cannot say what moves us.
As when we put our face to the wind
    Just because we want to.
As when we walk along the beach in winter

With only the gulls as company.
With the smell of salt on our lips
With the sun in our face
With the Almighty in our hearts
When we are alone together.
Let us dream a dream like this.
Consciously fashioned, deliberately pieced together; artistically structured.
Like a prophetic vision, like a 'seeing' or a 'hearing' which rings in our
souls and awakens us to a new level of seeing and hearing.
A dream like Redemption and Salvation
A dream like repentance and forgiveness
A dream such as God would dream.
Let this be our dream!
We *can* dream like this!
We *can.*

We alone on this earth have the power of expression in language, the ability
to transfer what we think and feel and know into appropriate categories that
others can experience along with us. That others can feel as we feel. That
others can know as we know. This is the proper power of man. We shall use
that power to achieve a mutual communication that is pure and undefiled by
any of the strictures of artificiality. We shall commune in a community of
common awareness that none but the "invited" can penetrate.
This effort shall be our dream.
It is not easy to dream a dream like this one.
It is not easy for many reasons, and all of them are valid ones. They are
reputed valid from what men have discovered in such adventures. Take
Christ, for instance. He dreamed a dream that was *so* fantastic, *so* un-
worldly (and everything that is un-worldly is fantastic), *so* devastating in its
consequences, *so* un-natural that
It sought to re-vitalize the whole world
That it sought to set men at odds
brothers against brother
That it would sanctify and underscore
Love.

Since the beginning of recorded history, men have thought about love. There are the epic poems of Homer and Virgil; the discourses of Plato and Aristotle; the countless experiences of the people who knew love but were not so well equipped to write about it. We have a whole, articulate man-kind to fall back upon to support our contention. But the question has always remained and vitally so!

"What does it mean to love?"

After all these years, do we, today, really know?

Do we still try to define it?

Do we still insert it into a logic that is
just artificially valid?
WHAT IS WRONG?

There *is* something wrong.

Of that we are all convinced. Literature and poetry; novel and song; voiced and emoted descriptions; — all these have fallen short of the mark, all these have failed

To move us sufficiently

To make us articulate

To inspire us rightly.

We say we love
BUT DO WE?

Whatever we say here is a trap. Humanly speaking there is no clear answer. And yet

In the intimacy of a thought

In the expression of a wish

In the fulfillment of a desire

In the ecstasy of a dream
WE KNOW THAT WE DO!

How do we know?

Because we "feel" it. Love is like that; it is felt. It is known deep within one's self. It is nourished in the privacy of our thinking — of our being. It grows to full stature in the expression of a nature. It is made public in the declaration of a soul. This is not mere verbalizing. Anyone who has loved or who loves knows what I mean. I mean what we cannot *say,* although we can *know* and *feel* and *experience* it. I mean what comes from the person in such abundance that it cannot be calculated.

Feel it and *you* will know.

This is part of a dream. A gigantic fantasy. A new and exciting situation. It is the envy of those who cannot love; the desire of those who do not yet love, but who want to, and can. This is the life of a man.

Let us re-live that life.

Let us re-tell it.

IN A DREAM.

Everything that is completely systematized in human life, sooner or later causes the enslavement of the individual. This can be done in the name of *government,* in which case the person becomes either a vote or a convenience. It can be done in the name of *family security,* in which case the individual loses his identity in the group of persons engulfing him in the fiction of human need. It can be done in the name of *religion* when worship is sanctified by a ritual which precludes singularity and makes a mere man to be the speaker of the voice of God. Systematization accepts no restricting bounds or limits; it recognizes no one specific area of competence; it knows no obligating law higher than its own highest obligating law.

In any system,

Men are fooled *or*

Men are imprisoned *or*

Men are deluded.

And yet, to Christ, all men were not just *all men,* but

INDIVIDUALS.

They were sanctified by the fact of their being individuals. They, as persons, were men. They were a redeemed people, bought by the sacrifice of God

Himself. The greatest heritage of Christ was the legacy to all men, of all time, that

> They were singular persons of undisputed dignity
>> They were articulate human beings
>>> They were sons of God and
>>>> "Heirs."

Perhaps the greatest obstacle to human expansion and happiness are the twin buttresses

> Of Language and
> Of Logic!

Without a doubt, these are, in any case, the distinguishing marks of what is *properly* known when men confront the most visible furniture of God's Universe. We — men — persons, speak and reason. At least, seemingly, within our present evidential framework, nothing else speaks and reasons. These facts, supposedly, identify the man as man. Yet, we must also consider

> His lowest identifying factor and
>> His basic distinguishing feature.
>>> That which is most evident to us
>>>> MAY NOT BE THE WHOLE STORY.

There may be something else, something important, something unique — which is not so specifically said. There may be something more, a bit higher, which is not so clearly noted. Man may be more than just a speaking and reasoning "something." He might be

> So properly personal
>> So distinctly individual
>>> So intimately himself, that
>>>> He, the person, could never be duplicated.

To be important though not important

> To be an individual though a member of a class
>> To be a person.

This alone is so meaningful. So forceful a thought. So explosive a concept.

Christ thought so, as He so often said, and so, by His Birth, Death and
Resurrection

We Are Redeemed.

To be "redeemed" means to be "bought-back-again."

It signifies that a price — a ransom — has been paid. It connotes a return to
an original situation. This is the most difficult of all mysteries in the
Christian Tradition. It is in the fullest sense incomprehensible, like the
Birth of Christ or His Resurrection. We cannot grasp it in a clear thought;
we cannot express it in a propositional form. This is, in the words of Christ,
"His Mission."

"I have come." He said, "to bring back sinners." Thank God that this was His
Mission. Were it anything less, then I would not have been included. In point of
fact,

Just who is the sinner?

I am the sinner, and for so many reasons.

For my pride, which dislocates me in this universe of reality

For my humility, which is the spoken lie to what I am

For my purity, which is only clean on the outside

"Like the whitened sepulchres."

If I could, in conscience and honesty, take a true account.

If I could be as impartial as the computer, If I could be as logical as the rules
of logic command, If I could look at myself, as I *really* am, If I could make
the act of self-consciousness to be another level of awareness wherein I could
observe, with precision and accuracy, the constant flow of the moments of
my life — If I could do all this, then

I would truly

Know Myself.

Sins are not "sins" like the words in a catechism, nor is even virtue such. In the
constant flow of life, in the world in which I dwell, in the certitude of my most
certain convictions, I know differently.

I know this from the heart:

That sin is separation from the Source of everything
That sin is not *just* a negation
That it is not just the absence or lack
Of moral being.
Sin is a doing, an acting, a performing.
It is to re-create the pattern of things
According to my image. But
I do not *make* the image.
I Am The Image.

To be good or holy or true; to be submissive to the command or invitation of some other; to be able to say "No," when I so want to say "Yes"; to wish, and mean it, that "my right hand reveal not its activity to my left" — this, and this alone is what it means
To be holy!

I am an existential fact, in all the complexity of that situation. I am a "being" in all the richness that such an event envisions.

The clarity of my own shortcomings notwithstanding, the devisiveness of my own identity undistinguished
I am a person
Redeemed and Sanctified
In the Blood of Christ.
I am a sinner.
In the Gospel-sense, that can only mean that
I Am Sorry.

I am sorry.
This is not just something to say; something to mutter when I am confused.
This is a confession — a *confiteor* — a revelation of self. The holy man is the man who knows in his heart
That he is not holy.
Who knows himself for what he is.
Who is *so* aware of his shortcomings.

It is not enough to say, "I am a sinner"; not enough to protest, "I am not worthy." It is not enough to declare, with all our hypocritical world, that, "Only God is Good." Certainly, it is true, and only too true, that God alone is good; but, when we say it, we must mean it with all our hearts.

There are many types of fool in this universe which we inhabit. There are the really ignorant; there are the simply un-taught, who are ignorant but not in the sense that we ordinarily mean; there are the supposedly "learned," who are *not* learned, but, who think they are; there are the docile who expect to be termed "smart" even though they are not smart; there are those who hide under the mantle of God — when the mantle is not borrowed from God but stolen.

Who in the world is worthy?

Who is holy?

Christ called a little child and said,

"Of such is the Kingdom of Heaven."

The child is important.

He is docile,

He knows his limits,

He does not put on.

NEITHER SHOULD WE.

To be holy, in the sense of Christ, is

Not to deceive ourselves

Not to delude others

Not to fool God.

It is not to sit in comfort

When others want,

It is not to demonstrate with posters and signs

To have our pictures taken.

It is not to wear an apron in an OLD AGE HOME

When a photographer is paid to enhance our image.

Banish the thought!

This is not Christ. Picture Christ that way and you have distorted the Gospel. Try to imagine the "Birth in Bethlehem" and you will see what I mean. Who of us lives in a stable and wants it? Who of us is cold without complaining? When do we seek out the poor and the weak in preference to the rich and the powerful?

Such a Christian lives a lie; and if he is smart at all, he knows it.
Color and rank and position so heeded
> Are the ministry of the Ambitious.
Not so Christ! He came, "Not to be ministered unto
> BUT TO MINISTER."

There is so much beauty in the world. Along with
> The ugliness
>> The distortions
>>> The mis-conceptions, that we encounter
>>> In living.

We are all basically so shallow. We look at the sun and *just* blink. We gaze at the stars and *just* gaze. We feel the chill of a cold wind and complain about it. We live through season after season, and that's all there is to it. As in the dressmaker's shop, the pattern has been established, and we take it as it is.
The beautiful gesture of a generous act
> In someone mal-formed
The clarity of vision openly displayed
> In someone blind
>> These things we read about and accept
>>> But *never* reflect upon!

The language that we speak, with all its variant sounds and accents. The sensations that we experience, with all their varied intensities. The thoughts that we think, with all their myriad meaningful-nesses. It is hard to express these self-intimacies, for they are so personalized in each of us. We can only point out what we feel in ourselves and look for others to see it in themselves. There is a whole world in every human glance; a universe in every human

encounter; there is a 'heaven' in every human act of love. And that is the answer
to the Scripture question.

"Who Are Men That You Are Mindful Of Them?"

Who are men? They are the "salt of the earth." They are the salt itself such
that if they "lose their flavor," there is nothing they can again "be salted
with." How could Christ say this, "You are the salt of the earth?" Do you
know what that means?

> It means that You season the universe
>> That You blend the end-less variety of events
>>> That You prepare what
>>>> God Himself tastes.

Christ did not just speak. He spoke with meaning and authority. He spoke in
the light of a majesty that ignorance has always tried to imitate. The ignorant
have always acted this way.

> In the presence of talent
>> In the presence of what is professional
>>> In the Presence Of God!

Just because we speak, we do not sound like Richard Burton. Just because we
punctuate, we are not even close to the mythical Professor Higgins. Just because
we live, we are not like

God.

> As we are, we are at once precious and worthless. "Remember son that you
> are dust"; and "You are just a little less than the angels."

In the logic of Faith, both statements proudly assert

> And assert correctly.

Like the Publican in the temple, bow your head in "humble" pride and say —

> "God, be merciful to me, the sinner"

Who can hear a thought, or feel a desire, or duplicate a pain?

> Who can fear as I fear without fear?
>> Who can cry my tears?

Only I can do these things. Only I.

No man can be ME. Nor can I be any other person.

I am myself — in the

    Prison of my own self

        The darkness of my own seeing

            The cave, where I dwell.

A garden of Eden. A Camelot. A Perfectness. This, in my world, is not so.

    I am a pilgrim, a wanderer, a traveler, who

        Intermittently seeks

For the next refuge.

    Christ was so like this.

        So like Me —

            and You.

It rains or it snows or the sun shines. The world about me lives in its infinite variety of life. The plant grows and I grow and my consciousness — self-consciousness — is my only mark of distinction. "God is in His Heaven," the story goes — and I am here. I ponder, as only a man can do, and I become afraid. I fear the unknown and all that I look upon is unknown. I sit and wonder —

    and wonder and wonder.

    There is no one I can turn to. No one I can trust. I look at the people around me and the sight makes me tremble. Goodness is a dictionary definition and what I see makes no sense. People try to buy what cannot be bought. They try to trade what they do not have or possess. I mean

        Fidelity.

The world is ridiculous. It is a puzzle. It is a paradox. I try to fathom it. I try to understand it. I try to make it reasonable — and I cannot. I attempt to apply my logic, and it does not work. I feel alone and lost and

        THERE IS NO MAP.

    I look out again and it is all there. All the bloodshed, the killing, the injustice, the wickedness. It is all there. The murderers, the robbers, the sinners, the world

        AND MYSELF.

I am on a city street, in darkness, without security.
I am lost in a maze of uncertainties.
I have forgotten my way.
There is no one to
Show me.
God help me and I will see!
Be my strength and I will endure!
Shepherd me and I will follow!
Show me the way!
I have prayed this
And I pray it now.
Oh, God, be for me
My God
Always!

II.
SUCH IS "TO BE THOUGHT"

Did you ever ask yourself seriously, "What does a thought mean"?
I don't mean the college-classroom type of question. I don't mean the
answer given by us to a Philosophy Instructor, for we would not ask him the
question in this setting. This is not a question chalked upon a blackboard or
copied down in a notebook. A question so asked has a conventional answer
depending upon the teacher we have or the school we attend. This is not the
question I mean!

    I mean, more realistically, the question
        That a man puts to himself
            When he is reflective and
                Alone.

What is it that I do when I think a thought? What does it all mean?
Christ asked this question so many times in so many ways. Not in the
syntactical form of a sentential structure, but in the form of the "city-street"
talk which we try to forget in the attempt to be learned. I put my question
apart from the confinements of a David Hume or a George Berkeley; apart
from the mechanized myth of "scholastic" abstraction; apart from the
contemporary cynicism of those who worship language and then demolish
it.

I put the question in the ordinary terms of men speaking
    In the solemnity of a social encounter
        In the genuinity of an affectionate greeting.
        In the way in which we speak.

The fact is that I have thoughts in my head. I know they are there for I voice them in the tones and according to the rules of language. I speak them and you listen and for the most part
>Understand.

Whatever else it may or may not be, a thought is a thing of beauty. It is holy in the sense that it re-presents for me and to me; in the sense that it re-flects mentally whatever I encounter. It is sacred for it reveals to me in my awareness something that I know which is revealed to you in the structure of my spoken or written sentences:
Beautiful
>Sacred
>>Holy
>>>Like God
>>>>Without dimensional limits.
Because of the thought I can converse and unite my separate self in the community of dialogue which brings men together as nothing else, in the whole world, can do. It is a capturing, a possessing, an owning.

I think
>That is the conscious fact
I speak
>That is the linguistic fact
What is it that I think and speak?
>>>That is the Mystery.

The word which communicates the thought, according to John, is an identifying name.
>>"Christ Is The Word."

The concept, the thought and the word, how simple they are in Aristotle's logic. Nothing is confusing here. The word just signifies the thought. This is just a primitive question of signs. It is nothing more, nothing less.
>>Just a question of signs.

But is it?

    Is it just a question of signs?

        Is this *just* signification?

I speak, and I speak what?

    I think and I think what?

        Just words and thoughts?

           Or is it

SOMETHING MORE?

Poor George Berkeley! How we laughed at him! He said that for something to-be is for it to-be-perceived. Or for the knower to-be, it is just to-perceive. He was such a young man, when he said this. I have heard it said that he was immature or boyish. Only a child could think that all things were just the thoughts of God presently thinking them. I heard all the text-book refutations about his Idealism; I listened to them; I nodded in assent. I, too, laughed, when my teacher read from a manual — I laughed because he did. It was the thing to do — at least for me the ignorant and un-trained beginner. I did not know, not could I, that the teacher was the same as I. I unconsciously assumed his

Infallibility.

That was my mistake.

    I did not recognize an "insight." I did not know what a vision was. I did not realize how to offer a critique as an improvement. Now I am so very ashamed — not because Berkeley was right — and I was wrong. I am ashamed because I thought that in questions such as this, there could be a "right" and "wrong."

"In the beginning was the Word."

    John said this in the sublime office of one who has seen God. Of one, who

    has seen the Un-Speakable and tried to speak it for us, who speak!

"The Word was God."

He said that too understanding only too well the tautology, the sentential identification, which would render it mysterious to his readers.

But David said, "The Lord is my Shepherd."

These too are the verbal outbursts of the visionary. Do not laught here though. These are living words which paint more sharply than the colored brush.

God speaks an un-imaginable Word

And words spark the imagination

A soul sings an impossible song

And our ears hear it clearly.

"The Word was made Flesh."

What about that? How much sense does that make for the logician? But, then again, remember, the logician never makes "sense." By his own admission, he is interested in the formal structure of arguments — and nothing more. Does God have to make sense, when reality does not and does not have to? God let me see my own limitations before I decree limits on others!

Let me know that, although 50,000 & 50,000 are 100,000,

I do not have to count them to know it.

The simple things are so complex for me

The world, the universe, is so big

I am so small.

Never let me think myself to be big, when I am not — and know it.

You, God, are not big either.

You are just that —

GOD!

When you have sat and listened to a concert or to the musical plot of an outstanding play, have you ever realized that this too is a thought? When you looked at a wonderful work of art, and having seen it, felt up-lifted; did you ever stop to consider that this too is a thought? Have you ever read or heard read a poetic composition, and had your imagination inflamed and your soul raptured, and remembered that this is also a thought?

What is a thought?

What is a reality?

What is God?

If you can find it in yourself to answer these sublime
    inquiries;
If you can find the key to these un-understandable
    mysteries;
If you can do this, then and only then do you know
                What a thought is.

If you say that a thought is a conscious expression —
      Then you have turned the question into a
        statement
              BUT THIS IS NO ANSWER.
If you say a thought is a mental picture —
      Then you have verbalized an image
              BUT THIS IS NO ANSWER.
If you say that a thought is an abstraction
      Then you have psychologically confused me
              BUT THIS IS NOT THE ANSWER.
What in the name of Heaven is the answer?
              I JUST DON'T KNOW!
              NOR DOES ANYONE ELSE!

Living, like logic and language, is a game. It is played according to the rules
that have been established. Everybody accepts these rules. They must.
Otherwise we could not play the game. In the three instances of 'game',
however, there is this one difference. Logic and language are man-made games.
The rules have been legislated by men like myself. The process, of course, was
slow; progress was difficult; perfection is still to be achieved. In living, it is
different. Here
        GOD MADE THE RULES.
What Paul says is "written on our hearts"; what Moses received on stone
tablets; what Christ re-iterated again and again —
        God once commanded.
These were the basic rules of living. God-made rules. Rules that demand the
bent head. I can speak English or French or German (or like some I know,

speak them all). The only condition is that I learn the words and organize them as syntactically correct. In living, this is not the case.

    God makes the rules.

        I may study them. But if I want to live fully

                I must obey them.

There is no other way. Heart speaks; stone lives; Christ says again

      "Thou shalt love the Lord thy God

        With all thy faculties

      And thou shalt love thy neighbor as

                THY "SELF!"

When we say, "What is an equivalent"? what do we mean? Do we indicate a verbal consistency, which the dictionary verifies?

    I don't think so. We mean much more. We mean so much more. An equivalence in logic means a balance of truth-values. It marks a statement in such a way that another statement balanced against it, takes the same, the identical, values in terms of truth or falsity. The human difficulty starts right here.

What is true or false?

    What is right or wrong?

      Who is the Master here,

        Man or his words?

If I could just see Christ in the ragged robes of an itinerant Jew

    If I could hear His words in the dialect that He spoke

      If I could fathom, in His day, what he vocalized

        I would know the Message.

There is a sadness here, and I know not why;

    There is an "ending" here, and I cannot punctuate it;

      There is a "beginning" here and it does not start.

What is all this?

    Christ was tempted in the desert;

      We are tempted every day.

    Christ was judged in a court-yard;

Our judge is the daily routine.

Christ was killed and once for all, because He permitted it;

We kill ourselves, because we know nothing else.

The melody in our heads.

The story on our lips.

The conclusion which is a

JUDGMENT.

What do they really tell of?

They tell of violence and ignorance. They tell of the extreme illogic of the emotions of a man. They tell of history — repeated and repeated — of time, counted and re-counted. Of minutes, and seconds, and hours, and days, and years — and even of centuries — that record the story of myself and all other things. This is an

IGNORANCE.

Who is ignorant? I am. Whatever I know or feel; whatever I communicate or speak; whatever I understand or reason out logically; whatever such may be

I am so un-certain.

I am a man. I need God. I thirst for "faith." I pray for evidence.

God grant me this. For only this way

Will I confront YOU.

What is God?

I can only use the same word.

God is

GOD!

Questions, questions, questions!

They surround me

They occupy me

They disturb me.

It is a curious fact that the seeking person has far more interest in the questions he asks, than in the answers to them.

An answer is so final, so complete, so finished, like a grammatical period. The question, on the other hand, is always so vital, so urgent, seeking full complete-ness.

Even when we know the answer, even then
>>We continue to question.
Perhaps this is because our life itself is a question. Not in the
propositional form of a language assertion, but, more, a question in and
of the complexity of the situation of life. How many times do we say,
"Do you love me?" to one who truly loves us? We never tire of the
question even though the "Yes, I do," as an answer, is in reality
unquestionable. The question just makes the answer more real, more
vital, more present; it does not add to our store of knowledge, it simply
uplifts us. We want so to be uplifted; to be raised up; to be possessed.
This, perhaps, is why we question so much the very things we feel
certain of. Did not Christ three times in succession disturb Peter?

>"Simon, do you love Me?"

>He knew it.

>>And yet He asked.
To formulate our questions
>To seek constantly
>>To re-explore the already known
>>>This is the "real" person.
This is not the doubter's question: "If you are The Son of God
>Come down from the cross."
This is not the legal question in court-room precision —
>"Master, just who is my neighbor?"
These are the *questioning* questions which have but one historical answer
and are then forever dismissed — never to be asked again. The lover's
question, that of the believer, that of the seeker — these are *questioned*
questions
>To be asked again and again because
>>The answer, though known,
>>>Vitalizes us.
"Lord, who is the greatest in the Kingdom of Heaven?"
>"Lord, what more shall I do to be perfect?"
>"Are You the Messiah?"
Questions like these — echoing the heart from which they spring; declarative of

the love that prompts them; indicative of the affection which verbalizes them —
these are the *living* questions.
It is this way that I confront Christ and voice my commitment.

I can say, over and over again, with feeling and devotedness.
I can ask Him at every moment
"Lord, who are You?"
"Show me who I am."
To live is to breathe, not the atmosphere, but the breath of awareness. Do not
negate this by pointing to the rooted plant or the bulk of an animal or to your
bodily limbs. You completely mis-read me when you do. This is all the
concreteness of living,
not the fact.
To live is to be self-contained in a "self." To be a conscious identity. To be a
certain someone whose uniqueness cannot be re-made or duplicated. For me to
live is to be myself no matter how tautological the language sounds. It is to
communicate a "presence," "my presence." It is to utter a "self" which cannot
be uttered
But just shown.
To live is to breathe and know and love
It is to be intoxicated, not by wine but by excitement
It is to be drunk.
Not drunk as when the brain is stupified or dulled.
But rather
When the mind is raised to a level which just looks up
When the beauty of what I dwell upon is caught entirely
In one swift glance.
To live like this is not so easily described; it
must be experienced.
The body becomes a prison like Plato's cave. This is an ascension; a fulfillment;
a completeness; not so much living as "being-lived." It is knowing that there is
more to me than just "me." It is the realization that living is not just a being
"here" or "there," but a being in
Being Be-ing.

Christ promised, "I am with you always." It is a present-being-with-me. The past and future are the relations of sequence and change. The believer is; he was not nor will be. He is. If you see this, you will see the stupidity of dis-belief and uncertainty. Was it not said to us, "A man does not live by bread alone." No, Lord, help me see that "I live by the words that come forth from the mouth of God."

The Eternal in time and history

Has made a mockery of temporal sequence;

The ever-present Presence of Christ

Has un-divested space and its limits.

If you live in the measured continuity of time, you have missed the message of Christ. You are like a thing; not like a personal self. You have a "before" and an "after." You can be logically arranged in a pattern of events like the other things of this world, but, and this is the key — "You are not of this world." You may be in it, but you are not of it.

To live in Christ

Is to see that the moments of life just melt

Into this moment.

As you think your thoughts into being

So God thinks you in a creative awareness. Such for us is

To Be Thought.

The logic of Faith is to finally discover

That in Faith

There is no logic!

To be thought; to be a "Thought"; this is for me to be. Not just to-but to-be-fully. God, the Infinite Self-Consciousness, without limit and dimension, speaks His Word in the concrete-ness of men and things

"And the Word was made Flesh."

Christ was "Spoken"; I speak on a different level as "thought-to-be." The self-righteous will smile here. In their foolishly fashioned logic, they will exclaim that a thought is nebulous, for they will compare it with the human concepts they mentally express. They will confuse the message of "being-a-man" with the language communication of the message. They will hit their chest to refute their being thought. They will never understand. And why not?

Because this cannot be understood!
And they will not realize that. They will quote the wondrous words of Christ in the monotony of a pulpit recitation.

With no comprehension of the verbal charge
With no appreciation of the poetic expression
of the mystical
So much apart from Christ.

They make logical the linguistic contradictions that Christ deliberately proclaimed. They explain the words in the nonsense of making them clear. They distinguish and then justify the distinction in the twin names of common sense and clarity. They do all this, but just remember Christ insisted:

"Unless you eat the Flesh of the Son of Man and drink His Blood, you shall not live."

The people heard these words. Christ did not elaborate. He said, "I am the Living Bread." Some, we are told, walked away in the ignorance of understanding the words that were spoken, and so ignoring the message that was communicated. Christ was not speaking nonsense. The nonsense lies in thinking that He would. Peter was magnificent that day. Whatever else he said or did in his remaining days, his answer is an ever-present monument to his commitment to Christ:

"Lord," he answered, "to whom shall we go?
You have the words of everlasting life."

"And the Word was God."

This is the importance here; this is the value. This "Word" is not the sound in the dictionary sense. This is the incompleteness of speaking underscored by the brilliance of intuition; of divine immediacy; of divine Presence; to a simple man. In contrast to the lilies of the field and the birds of the air; in contrast to the richness of appearance that is discovered in all the things that fill up the void of space that we term the world; in the light of such comparisons as these Christ said so simply and directly, "Are you of so much more value than these?"

The Word of God died
   For the "thought of God."
      How blessed, how blessed I am
         To be fashioned in the Consciousness of God Himself,
        To be thought-to-be.

My identification is from God.
   What could there be more than this?
             Simply Nothing!

A smile or a gesture with the hands; A reproach directed to a loved one; a handshake or a wave of the fingers, to say, "How are you?"; or "How do you feel?"; or anything else that resembles a shared warmness — these signs and countless others are specifically human. Only men do them and find a deep significance in the doing.

   Just ask yourself
            What *are* they?

They are an expression, a revelation, an unfolding of the heart for one who cares. They are a concrete communication in a human society or family; they pass from relation to relation in an ordinary manner. If they are said or done in English, you will never translate them into another tongue with the feeling they have in ours. They are peculiar to our culture; so peculiar that they assume, in the universe of discourse, a uniqueness that we confront in the universe of factual happenings. This is the world, stamped in some unreal design by the men who inhabit it.

It comes down to this:
We are what we are.
   We are classed as individuals in a universal set.
     We are pluralized in our culture and inheritance.
      This is the social fact.

The religious fact, if we may so speak, transcends the social fact. Men are not different in this respect. They are the same. "Personality" and "Presence" and

"Self" are not so classed in the dimensions that grow out of geographic situations and regional restrictions.

When God thinks

the Thought is the same.

I may not like this; nor may I accept it. But Christ did. And that is all important for me. Color and shape; family and status; time and place; intelligence or the lack of it —

All these fade

Into insignificance.

The seminal source of all of us is the same.

It is

THE CREATING ACT.

The Paradise of Eden is long since gone. The paradox of dissimilar artifacts of speech, stemming from the natural-ness of knowing no longer command attention. The colors and cultures or different races are accepted — perhaps contested — but no longer questioned. All of it is just *there*.

If we are true to our instincts

If we revert to the status of the child

If we express our hearts fully

Then we will know.

Our seminal source is the same. Adam is a common father, for he came first. Christ is a common Redeemer, for He came in "the fullness of time." We are men, brothers, human persons simply because God, in His Omnipotence,

THINKS US TO BE.

I am a man. A person. A value. Looking to God, this is what I mean when I say in the excitement of being,

Such is "to-be-thought."

III.
SUCH ARE OUR HEARTS

How can a man really declare what is in him? How can he speak what he feels
so keenly, so acutely, so fully; which, in truth, he knows is incommunicable in
words? How can he say something which *cannot* be said?

This has always been a problem which neither grammar nor logic can solve.

This is not the case because they are actually deficient, but, rather because
we know so much more than can be said according to rules.

We must be constantly aware:

That communication is broader than language,

That what is communicated is the *message*

Not merely

The words of the message.

There is such a wonderful "warmth" that always goes with beautiful
things. It is like a feeling, and it is not that; it is like an emoting, and it is not
that; it is something more, something fuller, something more expansive than
I can convey, something that must be experienced by *you*, and by *you* alone.

It is something of which I am so intimately aware

Yet which I cannot, with clarity, explain.

It is something apart that gets inside us and somehow

Becomes a real part of ourselves.

I have that feeling so often.

When I confront Christ in His words or in His deeds; when I stand face to
face with Him in a Gospel passage or in some artful, personal Christian
embodiment; when I bow my head for shame because I have sinned and, though
repentant like David, I want to sing out my sorrowing self.

I have that feeling now as I write these words.

To live a Christian life is so beautiful an event
    To be a Christian is an inspiration
        To everyone who is privileged
            To realize *somewhat* its meaning.

The Christian life is like a "hello" and a "good-by." It is a unique greeting and farewell, which have been mixed together so thoroughly that
    While both are distinct
        Neither one can be separated.
                Ever!

The real reason for calling the Christian life an "event" is because it means so much. It has a pride and a consolation; a peace and an intimacy — to be discovered no where else.

It is a sacrifice and a pain; an anguish and a longing, which while indescribable, are so realistically known and experienced. "If the world hates you," He foretold, "I want you to know it has hated Me first." I, too, am part of that cosmic hatred. In the mystery of history, I, like all the rest, did not want a Message such as this.
    But
Oh Christ, in my heart I did, for
                I need You
And I always shall. Suffering sickens me
              ESPECIALLY YOURS.

The Christian life is symbolized by the Christian heart. This is not the bodily muscle nor is it the sentimental reproduction of the greeting card. It is the projection of a meaning in an isomorphic likeness that affection effuses in the sense of Pascal who spoke of the "reasons of the heart" as those personal "reasons that the mind does not know."

The Christian life is
    Proud with the pride of our Heavenly Father
        As our moments of living produce true maturity

Consoled in the consolation of the Cross of Christ
    Which tears and sweat and pain have fashioned.
An anticipated peace which only those who know real fear
    Can wait for in patience and prayer,
An intimacy which is so completely thrilling
    As lofty values alone can thrill.

When Christian walks, his step is always a hesitant one. His journey is un-
mapped in any geometric manner. His task is to seek a path-way between
    Fulfillment and Promise
    Beginning and End.

To live like Christ, is one long hour that seeks out a revealing moment.
Expectation is so like this — looking for the new in the wake of the old. The
step of Christ is a cautious step, for the walking-ground is the hearts of men like
us. Every heart, though familiar, is strange.
    For this reason, Christ
    DOES NOT RUSH.

His Message, His words, — all these are guarded and tense. We speak
to Him, less with our lips, and more with our inner-ness, to make our
response more clearly heard.
    GOD MUST HEAR US!

The solemnity and the peace that He promised us are the un-forbidden fruit of
so much providential preparation. The Christian heart, like the Gospel heart, is
always, paradoxically, heavy and light.
    The heaviness is a weight that is felt by me because of the suffering of so
many others who do not know why they suffer. The lightness is a breath
of air, a breathing in and a breathing out, an exhaling, for the words of
Christ are like a refreshing wind that dries our sweat and cools the heat
that worry generates.
    "Though our crimes bear witness against us" —
How often did Christ sanctify these words! So often, in fact, that the

beloved John could reassure us:

"Though your sins be as scarlet, they shall be made white as snow."
How, oh how, could this be done?

Only

"In the blood of the Lamb."

I am so heavy with gratitude in the haunting memory
Of so much done and left un-done and
Still forgiven.
I am so weightless in the conviction that I can succeed
To the measure of grace and ability
That God has given me.
But, in all honesty, stripped to the naked limits of my own soul, from the hidden recesses of my total consciousness, there is really only one Gift.
It is You.
You who are, as Peter said so well.
Christ, the Lord!

While the Christian lives, he is always directing himself to a real ending. This ending is the fulfillment of a promise. In the truest sense, the Christian is complete for
He has been formed in God's Image
With God's Grace
With God Himself, Who is
Christ!

To live is a precious experience, apart from the questions it raises and the answers we must learn to survive. To live is to mould myself constantly into a child of God. We must see, like Martha, that "only one thing is necessary." For this insight we must express in the full-ness of our life an eternal

Gratitude.

We must be eternally grateful in anguished articulation to all who have contributed to the basic fact that we do live.

Grateful to God Who
>Gave us the power to know Him and the freedom to
>>choose Him.

Grateful to Christ Who
>Loves you so much more
>>than you could ever comprehend

Grateful to the love-fusion of your parents which
>Produced the physical life
>>that could be so divinely elevated

Grateful to the privileged few close to God who
>Have blessed you with every prayer
>>that they have ever said.

The very lived-fact of being-a-person; of being here and now; of being myself; this is, in a true sense, just an hour which is ending. Soon it will be only a remembrance like childhood or yesterday. The endless encounters of the total sum of our personal moments fit together with a logic that stuns us; especially when we realize that only thinking and speaking are logical, and that so illogical is

>The life that we live.

There is a plan to it all though. It is not visible in our present living, because that is now going on. The clarity of our history does reveal a plan — one un-authored by us.

Whether we like it or not, our past makes sense. It is a sense that we did not put there, for it always appeared non-sensical. My career just unfolds somehow uniformly even in the light of the innumerable free decisions of mine which I always imagined charted it just for me.

I live my life
>In its being-lived.

I direct my days
>In their being-directed.

I freely choose
>In my being-chosen.

I fully love
　　In my being-loved.
My life begins and ends
　　　　"in a fulfillment."
Christ, help me
　　　　To realize this!

The Christian life is, paradoxically, not only an ending, as we have seen; it is also a beginning. "Beginning is such a romantic word; how much it arouses up in a sleeping imagination, in a dozing conscience. How many solemn feelings it inaugurates, how many classic pictures it paints in my mind. The Scriptures proclaim "In the beginning" in the startling revelation of creation; John announces "In the beginning" with reference to Christ, Whom he entitled the Word. It is hardly strange that the life of the Christian, while truly an ending, should also be

　　　　　　　　"Beginning."
Life is so many things to so many different people.
　　To the teacher, it is a class-room;
　　　　To the mechanic, it is a shop;
　　　　　　To the doctor, it is a hospital;
　　　　　　　To the lawyer, it is a courtroom;
　　　　　　　To the mother, a home.

To the Christian, whether teacher or mechanic, or doctor or lawyer, or mother, or whatever else it is that people do, life is much like an un-picturable "self" silently unfolding within the mystery that it consecrates. What we do is live and we call it life. It is happiness and failure; success and sadness; business and pleasure. It is the thousand other ingredients that, so well mixed together, spell misery, anguish and joy in one un-thinkable, unspeakable, unspellable word.

That word is

　　　　　　　　"BEGINNING."
Sooner or later, this impossible life begins to begin,

And for everybody.

I try to embrace ideals and they blossom within me;

I pass through one mystery only to confront a new one;

I lift myself by my shoe-straps to find suddenly that

I am uplifted.

I read the words of Christ, which I have read so often, and, like Paul on the way to Damascus, I am hurled down to the ground. The lock on the mystery is still intact but

I have found the key.

A whole new world is opening up for me with each minute that I live. It is a world so fantastically realistic that I could never have dreamed it — and yet I so would have liked to dream it, had I but known. The experience of the past is only a seed. But

What a seed!

A seed lives or dies so very often through care and neglect.

I have a history — so much to look back upon, but so much to look forward to. I thought I loved and understood. I realize now, as full grown, as mature, as developed, as a man, that I must now love as a child. After all that is

What Christ wants!

I have served Christ in the past, so I thought;

I must serve Him better now, at this moment.

I have grown high like any living healthy thing;

I must now grow higher.

Christ has a claim on me, but

I have also a claim on Him.

I am his.

He must be in me — in my heart and soul

NOW AND ALWAYS!

We all have ideals; the most precious is the one that Christ Himself gave us, which is the specific love of persons. The measure of my loyalty to Christ is the devotion which I show to my ideals.

I am being formed in Christ, for this reason,
I must act like Christ.
Christ is growing up in me, for this reason,
I must grow up in Him.
Christ is a cosmic mirror,
reflecting everything and
everybody, and ME,
I must reflect Him.

Whatever I might become, or strive to be, or
long to be!
Whatever position, great or small, that I might
achieve, or, ambitiously, seek to obtain!
Whatever.
I have the memory of my "hour" of living, of
being, of loving.
I have the memory of this "now," which could
never be forgotten.

Beautiful things always thrill me; nothing, and again I say it, nothing
thrills me more than the promise of Christ. It burns in
MY HEART.
This is the Christian heart; not because it is mine but because I want it to
be. I want it to beat within me; to vitalize me; to convert me. This is the
Christian heart only because Christ forms it. A heart — the symbol of love
and a muscle. This is not a mere picture, this is a divine
SEMIOTIC.

We are Christians, for, having heard Christ, there is nothing else we can be. I
have been burned, for He said,
"I have come to cast a torch."
This is His message.
It is meaningful

in the ambiguous clarity of intuitive vision. The logician will smile here; and I will smile back at him. I will smile the more broadly, for knowing is not restricted to reasoning; even he knows that. I smile because I have discovered what all the world of logic could never teach me. I smile because God speaks in a sound-less language which Pascal so brilliantly termed "the reasons of the heart." I smile because the myth of legendary "Understanding" has been exploded. Contradiction is a logical function, just as truth is a logical value. The first sentence of the *Tractatus* may well be a mystical vision and not a linguistic definition,

"The world is everything that is the case."

Cusanus spoke of "learned ignorance." This too is a mystical vision. I have no such vision. I have only the word of God's spoken "Word" —

"What you do to them, you do to Me."

When Christ came into the world, the "Eternal" was in "Time." This is a contradiction as any simple logic book will show. But, having read and "seen," just ask yourself, "Who is here, in time?" The answer is at once as bright as sunlight or as opaque as mud

GOD IS HERE.

We, the persons, who live by meanings,
    For this is the full flower of our thinking,
Cannot cope with this sort of statement,
    For this is beyond meaning.
We shall hear it said, somehow it is always said this way,
        with words and signs
We shall hear it said that the words of Christ mean
        something.
That they mean this or that, that they signify something, but
        Do they?

Christ is God.
That is all that can be said. The life we lead is God's "day," and He shows it to us. For we are men, and He is God. Thank God
        That He is God!

The Christian heart is boundless.

    But in a very special sense!

This is not a spatial "boundless," which is an impossible thought. Nor is it a logical "boundless" which is a constructed infinity. It is not even a mental "boundless" which is descriptive of the mind's unlimited scope to know and know and know. The heart has an identifying "boundless" which the Christian Message confers upon it. All this is

Symbolic.

The heart is just the "sign" of love

    It stands in place of love in descriptive phrases

        It is a linguistic expression standing for

Christian love.

To say that the heart is boundless is only to say

That love is boundless.

To say that love is boundless is only to signify

    That it is limited in its amplitude to

No Distinguishable Group.

Christ appeared in a moment of history. He just appeared. He just came. He made Himself to be a characteristic type; "He emptied Himself"; He symbolized the Jew. He identified Himself with the children of Abraham, Isaac and Jacob. When He was born there was a sadness, such as "Rachel mourning her children." When He died there was a sadness, such as a Roman "Soldier striking his breast because this was truly the 'Son of God.'" To all the world, He was a Jew. Not an especial kind of Jew, but, rather,

The One Who was un-taught.

    With the smell of fish and wine on his breath

        Without shoes or proper attire. But with

The Message of God.

Could this Jew love?

    Could He love so much?

        Could He be in His right mind?

The "aristocrats" could only believe, "He had a devil."

    Even though some of them did not believe in devils.

The Roman could only ask Him, "What is truth?" (and not jesting),
When he did not acknowledge truth.
Herod, in simulated royal splendor, laughed at Him,
As the stupid always do when they do not understand
And are fearful of admitting it.
Still Christ loved them all. Does this seem strange? To me it does seem strange, for I know so little. Like Thomas, "I have been with Him for so long a time and I have not known it." The unfamiliar is strange to me, and this kind of love, while the truest kind, if I analyze it deep enough, is what even my poor love
Should have been.
If logic is a prison, it cannot contain love. The heart cannot be strapped. The person cannot be de-personalized. It is as simple as that. How I should have realized the Christ was conceived and born, lived and died, and rose again for such a basic purpose. This is His aim, His commitment, His involvement:
To form the Christian Heart.
To make us love.

There was never a night like tonight.
In all my experience of living I have never met with anything like this. When you read these lines, I am sure that you will not see what I see now. It is not because I see more — it is only because there is tonight so much more to see. The moon is a flame tonight. It burns, not like the glorious sun, but with a glow. I can only see it as the reflection of a log in a fire-place; warming, soothing, filling. The clouds, outlined by this moonish orange-ness, are like cotton. Not the cotton that is bushy and absorbent; but a stretched cotton — stretched to the point where it reveals something hidden behind it. I can see behind it. I can make out the form of the universe. Not the "starry sky" of Kant; not the structured physical shape of the un-shaped heavens; not the blur of an endless eternity; not anything like this. What I see can only be seen, in the same way that what I love can only be loved. It is a picture of the un-picturable; a re-presentation of what cannot be shown. This is truly a vision. With the moonlight and the stars, with the fire of

emotional ignition and the softness of cotton clouds, I can see what I never dared to see

THE FACE OF GOD!

Tonight, just in being the night it is,
    Is a sermon.
The air in my nose and lungs, cold and warm,
    Is a Gospel Homily.
The wind of my forehead, like the words of Christ,
    Brings the blood to my face.
The chill, which I can only feel,
    Is a melody. Oh, Christ!

Thank God for You!

Oh Christ, if only we could know how many nights like this You felt. You, "through Whom all things were made," did You make this night with Your creating Finger? You Who felt dust and dirt; Who wandered; Who preached; Who gave Yourself for ME;
    Was tonight something like the night

Before You died?

The heart that You want formed in me
    The love that You want me to give
        The sacrifice that Your love demands
        The altar of death

Is in me.

The Christian heart; I want it so. I want it as I never wanted anything else before. I long for it with such a burning desire. I desire it with such a fullness of longing. Dare I say, "Give it to me?" If I say that, then I betray my ignorance. I say again, as it has been said so many times, "Show me the Father and it is enough." I am such a fool, why oh why must I constantly

PROVE IT.

The voice to Augustine said
    Tolle lege.

                        Take and read!
The voice to me says simply
    Saltem vide.

                        At least see!
You were so right when You said:
                "Only the child can see this."
I beg You, with all my being, make me a child
                With a grown man's heart.

An ocean is a vast expanse-
    This is the love of Christ.
A desert is an infinite, unclaimed "stretching"-
    This is the love of Christ.
                    There is this difference!
The ocean and the desert are im-personal; Christ is so divinely personal. He
is so Singular, so Specific, so Individual, so constantly ours, that He puts us
to shame for not knowing it. His identification is the Son of God; likewise,
His identification is each and every person I encounter. The scholar and the
tramp; the sophisticate and the dull; the wife and the prostitute; my Mother
and everybody's Mother; all these, and all others, who make up this world
of ours are the identification of Christ. This fact makes His Message so
unique. And why not? This person is unique; He has God's
                    Heart.

Such a heart, could it be mine?
    It has to be.
Such a love, could I possibly express it?
    I must.
Such a life, could I possibly live it?
    I have been commanded to.

This is not poetry, except poetry be the communication of fact.

This is not meaningless, except meaning be merely confined to words. This is not speech, except speech be a concrete commitment.

If I am one of those "of so little faith," then I too may foolishly doubt,
    "That I can do all things in Him who strengthens me."

Were Christ here tonight, before me, beckoning to me, would I rise up and follow Him? Would I leave all things and walk behind Him? Would I listen from a boat? Sit upon a hill-side? Chase the children whom He loved? Look at the Samaritan woman with such righteous mien? Run away when the Temple police seized Him?
    Lie hidden when He was nailed to the cross, naked? Disbelieve when it was reported to me that He had risen from the dead?
    What would I do, knowing myself?
                        The easy things!
    What would I not do, knowing myself?
                        The hard things!
That is why my heart must be formed
                    Like the heart of Christ.
That is why my love must flow and flow
                    Like the love of Christ.

The Christian prayer is such a simple one, for it is the prayer of a child. It is said in simple sentences which possess a "sense" that is un-analyzable; like a kiss or a hug or a squeeze of the hand. Did not Christ want it this way? It is in this manner we pray.

Lord, give me a heart like Yours
    Give me a love like Yours
        Give me a dedication like Yours.
In giving me all this,
    You will give me what I want —
                    YOUR HEART AS MINE!

IV.
SUCH ARE PERSONS

Wittgenstein wrote at the conclusion of his *Tractatus:* "That about which one cannot speak, one must keep silence." We, all of us, from the simplest to the greatest, know so very much; our mental content is so overwhelming, so extraordinary, so humanly marked, that we actually experience so much more than we could ever properly speak. We cannot speak a "pain," or an "ache"; we cannot properly speak the awareness of "self"; we cannot truly speak in language the depth of our love.

Language does not work here.

Still we must communicate;

We must make known;

We must proffer our knowledge.

And yet, somehow, in language, so simply voiced and spoken,

We Cannot.

This is indeed a problem. Let us reflect upon it.

Logic is my business, in that I teach it. I am affectionately dedicated to language in that I love it. I love its sound and its formation; I love the way it springs from my tongue and begins to live in the thought that it generates in another; I love what it says and how it says it. I have also a lived commitment to logic. I perceive a beauty in its structure and form. I am enchanted by its claim to validity, and the generative power it possesses to produce a "proof." This is just an expressed fact of my living, and yet

These are my prison.

I am bound by them. I am strangled by the love I bear them. I am engulfed in the infinite end-less-ness which they pour over me. Objectively, and not emotionally, this is to be a "prisoner of love," because I know so much more

than
I could ever speak.
I know things, but how poorly? There is nothing, it seems, that I know in itself.
The things I encounter, both conscious and unconscious, the persons I meet, my
family, my friends, those in general whom I love or like or have affection for —
all these are known.

But how?
I subsume them,
I integrate them,
I common-ize them,
Under a classification that
is universal, and so
Not proper.
There seems to be nothing I know precisely as this individual thing in itself
not even
My own self.
And yet I do know. I know in a way that is not entirely intellectual, as I have
been taught. I know in a way that is piercingly singular. Somewhat like a dog
who knows his master, but much, much, more so. I know you whom I love in a
special way; in a personal way that no one else could ever experience — because
it is
Just Mine.
In some such way, Christ knew people. He knew them inside and out. He
knew them completely. "He has told me all that I have ever done," said the
woman at Jacob's Well. In this way He knows me, THE PERSON. It is this
that I seek in His Name, such personal knowledge and
Its expression.
I talk to you and you talk to me. That is conversation, which is basically the
sharing of a self. It may be in the intimacy of a personal moment or in the unity
of a social group. Whatever it is it is a sharing and an expression of what is
shared. The wonder of Aristotle is the ambition of Christ; the mission of
Socrates, the knowledge of myself, is the invitation of Christ. The myth of Plato
is the sanctified parable of Christ. "Give to Caesar that which is his," did not

pertain to Caesar alone. This is the dedication of someone who is dedicated to Christ. He sends us

"As the Father has sent Me."

To be a person, in the meaning of Christ, is
To dream consciously and with design
To articulate clearly and with voiced command
To imitate Him of whom the centurion said,
"Lord, I am not worthy."

What do I really want? Peace?
"My peace I leave with you."
What do I most desire? Security?
"This day you shall be with Me in paradise."
What do I long for? Recognition?
"I lose nothing that the Father has given Me."
What do I thirst for? Salvation?
"I lay down my life freely for you."
"No man takes it from Me."

Why do we doubt? Troubled with cares and anxieties; burdened with the crosses that have no meaning; dawdlers in a herd without a shepherd. Poor Pilate, the governor of a second-rate province, confronted Christ and said, "I have the power to kill You or to free You." Christ merely answered what we know to be so obvious.
"You would have no power over Me
Were it not given you from above."
How many times have I myself seen Christ today and unthinking thought to exercise power over Him?
In the student who sat before me whom
I imagined was insolent?
In a loved one who questioned me and whom
I un-dignified as doubting?

In a subordinate, whom I, in my ignorance,
   Doubted?

How full the world is. How full of things and persons. How full of situations and hard facts. Unless Christ was wrong, all these are supremely important, not only in themselves, but also for me. I shall never be a Christian, until I recognize fully that a person, any person, is a "value in itself"; until I realize that any person has an importance that I do not give to it and consequently *cannot* take away from it. If I know myself at all, I will know what it is
   To be a person!
To be a person such as Christ demands is an almost inhuman task. Without Him and His Help who could do it? Peter walked with Christ; studied with Him as a student with a Master. He heard His words; saw His deeds; and knew Him in a personal, many-intimate, even intuitive, way. Yet, as with so many of us because of what we are, his comprehension was so limited. Christ had come to suffer and die; that was His Mission, and that alone. Yet, when He reminded His own people of this fact, they protested that this could not be. They would forbid and prevent it.
   They would prevent what! Something that was
   The eternal, inevitable plan of God,
   The Redemption of the world,
   SALVATION!

Was this the perverse and un-believing generation? Was this the "get thee behind Me, Satan?" Am I the one who "comprehends so well the thoughts of men
   But not those of God?"
Make me the person that You desire to sup with. So that when You knock
   I will know You and open the door.
Make me the person who, when so heavily burdened
   Feels Your refreshment.
Make me one who accepts his day's wages and looks at no one else
   To question Your generosity.
Make my heart burn within me when You speak

> Like the men on the way to Emmaus.
> But do not vanish from my sight.

This is the Christian person. The one who just loves because it comes to him naturally. Who believes because he could never suspect to doubt. Who hopes in the fullness of the certitude that comes from the Gospel words. This would be a man

> Strong like Samson
> Brave like David
> Wise like Solomon
> God-like as was Christ
Who was, and is, and will be forever and ever
> God!

Oh Christ, look into my heart so that I,
> Like the Samaritan woman, can shout to the whole world
> Loud and strong
> With true conviction
> Seared with God's glance
"Come with me and see one Who has told me everything that I have ever done"

Let me not worry about where to worship; let me just fulfill Your words so that, I, as You so desired, might come to see that
> I worship God, "the Father
> In Spirit And In Truth"

The more I read and contemplate, the more I understand and estimate, the more I remember and realize, so much the more do I recollect on what should *not* have been, what never was intended and was, what is abominable to Christ and still is. I think
> Of the pompous theologian who dogmatically declares,
> Of the self-righteous religious who thinks garments make for status,
> Of the ignorant academician who binds men with the past,
> Just for the sake of tradition.

I shiver as I think of the gentle Christ,
   Who in His Divine-ness,
      Loved all men enough to die for them.

What would He say today? How would He feel? How would He react?
Words can be an intoxication! The beautiful sounds of language that have
developed to the position of literature. Which have made beauty come alive
in sounds and sentences, in poetry and song, in the ordinary greetings which
include God. Like an aged wine, with the delicacies of the table, words can
console, and delight and uplift.
               But, on the other hand,
What a terror they can be!
If ever a mere human speaks words, as though they are the words of God
Himself,
      If ever he tries to give meanings to the words of God which are so meaningful
                     In themselves.
                     This is disaster.

The man who claims to be a Professor, when he is not
   Who says he loves the academic, when he is not capable of such love
      Who claims he teaches merely because he speaks and re-peats
         Second-hand thoughts.
Such a man could never confront Christ.
   Only the coward would assume a prominence because of an accidental social
   standing. Only a fool would claim to be important, because no one is. Only
   the devil would quote Christ to support what he does not believe. The true
   man quotes Christ because he believes what He says and then practices its
   necessary consequences.
But to construct a moral logic,
   To distinguish for convenience,
      To justify an end with a "holy" means,
         To shout "Deus vult,"
            When God doesn't . . .
This is a mockery.

The hypocrite is an abomination.

He secretly practices what he publicly condemns.

He loves justice but winks at "official" injustice.

He loves the poor but only in words.

Christ exposed such as this to underscore His Message. I shudder to think that those who follow Him, in the name of His Message, crucify Him

Day after Day.

Who is the Christ-like man? What an earth-shaking question this is. How, perhaps, unreasonable is it to ask it? The Christ-like man is the man like Christ, and that is so tautological — so like saying that all black dogs are black. Or is it?

In logic a tautology is a sentence that merely repeats itself, such that actually it says nothing. In a formal construct the tautology is the basis for proof. It is the foundation for erecting a systematized demonstrable structure. Within the framework of language, wherein the "message" must be distinguished from the "communication," we can mean more than we actually say. Therefore, and with meaning, the statement — "The Christ-like man is the man like Christ" — does communicate.

It says something;

It means something;

It creates an atmosphere in which there comes clearly

An Intuition.

I heard a preacher today. I heard him deliver a prepared talk. I heard him, in underlined humility, proclaim his fitness to declare the Message of Christ. I listened in intellectual disgust to his platitudinous phrases. I looked within myself, and, in an immediacy of vision, asked myself, "Could this be I?"

Who is anyone to pass judgment? "God alone judges."

WHY?

Because God alone, in His unfathomable wisdom,

"Sees into men's hearts."

To say, "I believe that Christ is here, now, present," is wonderful, if

I know what it means.

To say, "History teaches us the way to the resolution of the questions of today"
is fine
> If I know what history means.
But, if I know nothing, then God help me
> I should say nothing.
>> That *would* be humility.

The man of Christ says with a heart full of self-knowledge,
> "I am not worthy"
>> Simply because it is true.
>>> He is not.

But how worthless are the words and their kin-like sentiment, if we become
annoyed
> When someone else, in a simplicity of soul,
>> Not only agrees with us but tells us *why*
>>> We are unworthy.
The Christ-like man is not a thing of beauty
> In a splendor of dress,
>> In an elegance of appearance,
>>> In a figuration of fragrance.
He is like Christ, whom Isaiah so well described, as
>> "The most abject of men."
Give us such a man, and we will see Christ, our Lord, for
>> "By His bruises we are healed."
Men cannot be classified. The psychological types, so easily available in the
corner store libraries, so quickly quoted in the social gatherings of the common
elite, so knowingly applied in that privacy with our special friends, tell so little.
If we could only be true to life and see others as we wish them to see us. We are
not like plants or stones, like flowers or animals, like "things" which
> Because of a physical configuration,
>> Because of a color or shape,
>>> Because of a measured observation,
>>> Can be translated into a statistic.

Men are persons, and persons are unique. This uniqueness lies in their self-
ness, which can never be duplicated.

We may look alike;

We may be alike;

But we are just "ourselves."

There are times in our experience, in our personal confrontations, in our
intimate meetings, that a certain person will stand out. He will exemplify, for
our minds and for our hearts, some ideal which we have fashioned in our brain.
Some picture, which, if we could paint, we would commit to canvas to *show*
what we mean. As I reflect here now, I recall such a man. Let me briefly
describe him, perhaps you knew him too in the countless mass of persons you
have met.

Though it is unimportant, this man's name was Luigi Bosio. An Italian
who became an American. An immigrant whose accent constantly betrayed
his origin. He was a gentleman, a Christian, a Priest. In all the truth of my
heart, I can really say, "He was a man." He was never honored, never
praised, officially downgraded. He was funny, if you call funny that which

Makes you cry.

He was intelligent, as is the peasant

who examines the soil.

He was generous in the most special use of the word,

Like Christ,

He gave himself.

Unlike Christ, he had faults. But, as Christ-like

He admitted them.

In the two decades, minus three years, that I knew him, I grew to love him.
It was a love that was symbolic which resists translation into the categories
of the language terms of endearment. He was like

Zacchaeus, small in stature, but not nearly so rich;

Joseph, except that he had no physical Mary;

John, except he had no mystical view.

He gave a sermon in a shrug. He lectured wonderfully with an in-
stantaneous sigh. He turned the other cheek. He prayed, he loved, he
sinned, he forgave and sought forgiveness, he was sorry that he was not

better, and, this alone, made him better. God finally called him: he died, and he was buried; and he was so quickly forgotten. I know that he is with God, not because he was without fault, but because he knew it. I shall never forget him, please God, because he was such a man

A Gospel Person.

More than this, no one can be. The great lesson of Christ is here concretized. It is the fact that

Life has a lesson

And it is through people, and only through them, that we

Come to know it.

To know and to be so certainly aware; to understand and to reason with the guarantee of validity; to sit and to contemplate as a Master

The whole world.

To let thoughts roll into our heads
    Like the shore receiving the ocean's tide,
To have feeling and to feel a pain
    In the citadel of my own self,
To be in intellectual anguish
    Confronted by the meaninglessness of meanings,
This is to be a man —
    Fully
        Without doubt
            In deepest certitude.
It means to be a person. It means to live a life. For the individual life is the complexity of all these disconcerting elements. None save the person could make this claim with a longing —

Who else would want to?

The filth and beauty; the stench and fragrance; the un-ending toil and the thrill of fulfillment — all this marks off the individual life.

    Does it all have a total meaning?

    Does "meaning" itself have a meaning?

The question seems logical in its abstract formulation, but in the singularity of my "lived" life, it is far from logical. Living can be forced into a logic but only at the expense of living.

To be smart or stupid in varying degrees
    To be beautiful or ugly in graded intensity
        To be such that I am accepted or rejected by others
These are common characteristics which develop from the accidental sources of
                        Heredity or Talent.
        To be one of these, as an individual, may be a quality of a man; but to be
    a man, a person, is not to be *just* one of these. The man is so much more
    — like the relation of species to genus, he is a full-ness; a perfect-ness;
    and most of all a
                        "Nothing."

What is there about "Nothing" that intrigues me so? Could it be that there is a "something," a distinguishing feature, about "Nothing"?
                        How could this be?
Complexity always serves to dissipate, whether in thought, or in being, or in action. Simplicity, on the other hand, serves only to unite.

The simplicity of my thinking unifies the raw data of consciousness;
    The simplicity of my loving is my union with a person;
        The simplicity of my being is to see God.
"Little children," Christ called us. What, in the whole world, is more simple
                        Than they!

How much more enticing and satisfying is an invitation than a command. This is most fully to recognize my man-hood and personality —
                        To be invited.

The Message of Christ is an invitation. To be sure, it entails commands; but it is first an invitation. The commands are articulated, only when the invitation is freely accepted. The beast and the slave are *just* commanded; they are owned

and used and even sold. For a man to be *just* commanded is a disgrace! The
person is always special,
    Much more than an event even though always
                "Less than the angels."
Events occur, but persons live. He has to live his life in a full-ness; in a
completeness; in an entirety. To be fooled is common to all conscious beings;
but to fool one's self is proper only to man
                    The person.
He is the one who can look knowingly at the heavens,
    Who realized the infinity of life beneath the sea,
        Who can look at an eagle soaring high,
            And is glad that he walks.
He is glad because he realizes only too well that he walks up-right.
    In walking, he is so close to the earth, the source of life,
        As up-right, he steers himself towards the heavens
                The promise of more life.
The "Christian" person is the greatest of cosmic paradoxes:
    To become a man he must first be a child;
    To become a child he must first be a man.
"Unless all of you become like little children" . . .
                Are the words of Christ.

V.

EACH MAN IS AN ISLAND

I want you to look with me; to take a good look; the kind of look that you must prepare yourself for. The kind of look that looks "into" and not just "at." I offer the invitation to examine, without microscope or measuring instrument, just what we live in. I not only invite you to do this; I defy you to do it. I do not want you to look into yourself, at least not now, just to look into what we live in. To do so is a revelation.

To look at the sky and see it for what it is —
    An infinite infinity.

To look at the sea, not as a rolling ocean, but as
    A mother sheltering a teeming variety of living things.

To look at the mountains, and the city streets, and the valleys, those natural temples so un-like, and yet so like, the Temple in which
                    Christ taught.

Then just ask yourself, "What does all of this mean?"
    All my life I have been flooded with torrents of meanings. Meanings in my head, and in the things about me. Meanings that I conceived, and meanings that I have discovered. Meanings that mean something, and meanings that mean nothing. Meanings that have value; and meanings that are value-less. I have searched for meanings, constructed meanings, dissected meanings, and even discarded meanings. This was a philosophic quest for me. It was an attempt to live fully a lived-life. I constantly asked myself, "What do I

mean?''; ''What does he mean?''; ''What does this or that mean?'' I asked
myself so often and the answer was always, though I didn't realize it,
Without reward.
This is only to say that my answers to the questions of meaning were themselves
Without meaning.
It seems incredible!

Yet this, and this alone, was the case.

It seems ridiculous!

Yet it wasn't ridiculous; it was the case.

Meanings, sometimes, could be
SENSELESS!
What, after all, makes sense? The world in which I dwell is a totality of
meanings and I encounter them day after day. The classes of things; the
members of those classes; you and me, and whatever else can be so designated,
all embody some type of meaning. Yet in the total set-up; in the conglomeration
of meanings; it all seems
SO ABSURD!
The absurdity of life and death, of sin and virtue, of struggle and fatigue, of
constantly searching, — searching for what?

To live?

I do live.

To die?

I shall die.

To be?

I am.

I have all this, I know all this. Sometimes I realize all this —
THAT I NEED SOMETHING MORE!
What is "something more?" What is it I am commanded to bow to?

It is just You
Oh Christ!

There is nothing — nothing in the universe of discourse, vast as it might be;
nothing in the endless realms of critical logic or ordinary language; nothing in
the recorded history of events long since past; nothing in the un-speakable world

of thoughts, or of things or of happenings; nothing even in the indescribable ecstasy of real human love; nothing, just nothing, has any meaning at all apart from

YOU!

I am young and I am old,
   I am unlearned and I am learned,
      I am foolish and I am wise,
         All this, and so much more,
            In one lifetime.

Mine.

I want with all my heart to see, because I know it, that
   It is such a tragedy just to live,
      Just to breathe the air I need,
         Just to feed myself and to grow,
            Just to think, and to will, and to explode
my most basic emotions
   When I do not know YOU.
To know YOU, as You said so well, is the only way for me to be

A Man.

I do not know how else, but to be a man is to live, and to live fully.
   I must be lived
      By You;
   I must be willed
      By You;
   I must be loved
      By You.

This alone is my sanctification, my full-ness, my holiness, my plan, and my destiny. In this atmosphere, there is no sin, no dis-order, no meaningless meanings, no sense-less speaking. No, for You have enriched it all. You have fashioned the universe and You have thrown me into it. This universe, which by itself is a sense-less-ness, hits me with a force that staggers me. Then You throw the key to me to unlatch the mystery. I face up to the mystery with this key, for now I can unlock it. It is now, and only now, that I see clearly. Now I can see and now be quieted — for, though I always knew it, now I realize it so well, so clearly. That key that was given to me was

JUST YOU.

The fallacy that there "exists" a mankind has for too long been exploited. We are compressed into a family-ness — a patriotism — a nationalism by others who use these labels to achieve self-enhancing goals. We have become part of a crowd, of a group, of a national circle, that is not "really" real. Pilate said to Christ, "Am I a Jew?" — Christ never said to Pilate, "I am a Jew." Race and background, properly placed, have great cultural value. Improperly placed, they are dangerous and so value-less. A man is not of this place or that place — of this blood or that blood — of this kind or that kind. That fact — just this fact, that he is a man

Transcends these limits!

Each person, on his own, is an identity
    Has his own unique being
        Is just himself and

No other!

My identity is more than my name.
    It is more than my family origin;
        It is more than my social status;
            It is just, and no more, the tautology
"I am me"

This at once says everything and says nothing. The logical contradiction — or contrary — reveals the physical, existential fact that
    To be is to be myself. And just that!
        Not in the identity of a physical sound
            Nor in the figuration of a geographical strain
            Nor in the stature of a specific culture
            But only in this physical something
"Me"

No man — no person — no human being can be so systematized that he loses his precious, sacred identity. From the moment of the creative act which made Adam and Eve to be what they were — each person is in himself a definite somebody. More so — since the redemptive act, wherein God made an infinite but definite purchase, by the giving of Himself — ever since and for always

You are You
I am Me.

Take a piece of soil in your hand and look at it. I don't mean "dirt" in the ordinary sense, I mean "ground." Look at it with the naked eye. You see blackness and depth and smell the pungence. You look with the eye of a man — not microscopic, not scientific, not mechanically like a computer — but like a man. You see it and you feel it. It is moist and clay-like — it is dry and flaky — it is just a lump in your hand. No matter how long you examine it, it is still dirt and it is dead.

But is it?

Look again! Is it conscious? No, For it gives no evidence of such awareness. Does it live? No, For it is *not* alive such that it grows and reproduces. As we see it, it does not live. Yet just think!

This is the mother of cosmic life;
This is the germinal source of being;
It is here that the seed is dropped
Which grows and lives.

This is what Christ spat upon
    To cure blindness;
This is what Christ slept upon
    To regain His strength;
This is what Christ walked upon
    To fulfill His mission;
This is what God held up to address all men —
    "Remember, Son, that you are dust and you shall return

Unto dust."

Such a lesson is here for us to learn! Such a textbook of nature!

From what does not live
  Living things spring forth;
From what does not breathe
  Breath is made possible;
From what seems to be just "there"
  Teeming life is present.

Like Christ Himself saying "Unless you die, you shall not live," for, "I have
come to give my life as your redemption." Like the soil, the Word of Christ is
here. Christ who Himself died — but only that
                    "I might live."
There is such a magic in words — such a force and a feeling — such a
mental movement — that all too often we treat words with a tolerance so
much below their dignity. I would call that dignity regal — but that is not
correct. Words, in any sense, *are* ordinary. They are just articulated sounds
which vibrate from our mouths with a de-tonated meaning. They move,
they inspire and sometimes they crush us with a force that we cannot parry
— which leaves us at times helpless and vulnerable — both for good and for
bad. I am thinking at this moment of the word
                    "Creation"

Apart from the dictionary sense,
    Apart from the language usage,
        Apart from the sanctified "logic" of those who speak for God,
            What a word this is!
It un-nerves us, it shakes us, it prompts an impossible thought. In the full self-
possession of real sobriety, this word
                    Intoxicates me.
It numbs my brain
    And brightens my vision;
It locks my throat
    And comes out strong and clear;
It confuses my mind
    To produce a clarity

That lights my mind. This is

CREATION

I have said it is an "un-thinkable" thought. That is true. But the un-thinkable can connote on so many levels.

It may be the non-sense of "nothing"

This is a verbal and mental emptiness.

It may be the non-sense of "something" which though not graspable in the ambit of a thought is nevertheless "meaningful" in an experience that is

Un-thought.

Love is real — but we cannot think it — we cannot picture it. We cannot voice it except in the feeble expression of some language term. We can sing it — but we cannot say it. We know it but we cannot image it. We can share it, and share it we do, but here the sharing, the communicating is

Love Itself.

To see something in the full clarity of a clear vision. To know something so very personal and proper — but not be able to say it — to feel something and, chained to a logic of discourse, be unable to deduce it. This is a vision.

Creation too is a vision — but this is

A Vision of God.

To describe it in Man's words is an impossibility,

To attempt to define it is

An Absurdity.

To accept it is

A Christian Birthright.

VI.
TO BE FORGIVEN

The splitting up of any language in terms of tense with its past, present and future, makes it so very difficult to apply the words of speech to the fact of God. There are so many questions raised and thus:

So many problems formulated. So many solutions imposed upon people. For what end? They serve

No purpose.

The reason for a past and a future really depends upon the necessary present. We live in the present — we mature in the present — we die in the present. For us to look backwards or to look forward is just

A manner of speaking.

Is not even "time" an abstraction? Just think!

The fact that

this happened or

this will happen

is rooted in the

"Here and Now."

To escape the present is unthinkable. To live the past is a delusion. To live in the future is rank foolishness. How strange it is that language should so engulf us as to completely immerse us in such an artificial ocean of words. To say that logic is a prison is comprehensible enough, for, in reality, everyone knows that we construct it. To say that language is a prison is not so easy to see, for we are in a certain sense born into it. Nonetheless, language too is a

Prison.

It is like proving this or that — like showing that this happened or that happened, or that this will or will not be. Such a device must needs borrow from history, for history is the articulate witness to demonstration and often

Deception!

Does God speak?
    Is this a question that can be raised?
And, if so, why?
    And, if not, why not?
It is so sad a plight to be completely immersed in language, and not to realize it — as if language was the end-all — as if there were nothing else. The world continues to suffer from the substitution of words for things,
    of black for a certain man,
        of white for another man.
When, as we all know, what man denotes — to say nothing of connotes — is somehow colored, but really in meaning it is

Color-less.

Men of wisdom have spoken about this. They have called it the question of Reality and Appearance. Is this really *the* problem? Or is the problem better still

Appearance and Appearances?

Something is short when it is seen in terms of one comparison and long in terms of another. Someone is smart relative to this person, and stupid relative to that person. Contemplative men have said this so long ago — we nod our heads and agree and go away

Un-moved!

Christ said that unless our justice exceeds that of the Scribes and Pharisees, we shall be lost. Does this mean that the Christian must be more "just" because the Scribe is less "just"?

Hardly!

Just as the Christian "Child" is not merely the physical embodiment of his many attributes but rather the spiritual subjection of the Person in love and trust! There is always a polarity of balance in the"Measure" of God.

From the outside it looks absurd.

Spoken, it appears sense-less.

But having been believed, the measure *has* meaning.

If hope were founded upon evidential knowledge, we would all despair. Hope and love follow a higher conviction than personal experience could ever permit. This is the experience of God which is shared by us through faith.

Oh, Christ, I must

believe like the Child

to follow like the Lamb.

If strength were something like an arm or a leg, the cripple could never be strong. If love were centered in understanding, the child could never love.

And yet the child does love!

It is so easy to condemn the harlot who sells herself for money; who condemns by name the man who pays the money to use that self. The harlot washed Christ's feet, and Christ was condemned —

Not because of what she was

But because of what He was.

This is the logic of the world — to seek out the easy way, and to make this the way of righteousness and justice. Thus, we can absolve the past with a promise for the future, and we can cover over the base-ness of a deed with a resolution that we pledge to fulfill. It is the old cry —

"It is better for one man to die than for the whole nation to perish."

It was for this reason ultimately that Christ died. From that day to this one, and, in God's Holy Name, how many other singular men have died for mankind?

Yet

The individual alone is real;

"Mankind" is just an abstraction.

How many times have justice and goodness and virtue of any kind been re-interpreted by a jumble of words? Christ said, "I am the Truth"; they called Him a liar. Yet, they could show no lie that He spoke. Christ said, "I am without sin." Yet, they said He was a sinner. Still they could show no sin that He committed. Unless

It is a lie to prophesy, or

It is a sin to sit with sinners!

But this is the way of the world! To sit in solemn judgment and to say, without truly meaning it, that we are not fit to judge. Pilate said it so well, and all of us constantly echo his words.

This Man has done nothing, "therefore I shall punish Him."

Pilate is not in the past. He is here speaking for every man who is a hypocrite. As Pilate speaks, in much the same way the world through Him speaks

For me!

Every problem has a solution (or so we are told) ignoring meanwhile the possibility that the solution itself may be as much a problem. How many times are we so articulately told and re-told the problems of life, when for all practical purposes, the only problem is that of

Being a man.

The Christian alone has the solution to this problem. That is why, in all the glory of speech and the mystery of being, God became Man. It is not always fashionable to talk of this mystery, or, for that matter, any mystery. Perhaps the greatest mystery of them all is that we should seek so hard

To avoid mystery.

Yet, the enigma of living,

The power and glory of national monuments,

The sophistication of learning,

The very emptiness of all human patterns,

All these have no single key to achieving holiness

Apart from Christ.

Yet, who — how many — listen to Him? Even we, of all the Christians, close our ears. For that reason the Finger of God is pointed at us in the sad commentary that

"Hearing we do not hear,

And seeing, we do not see."

Christ, ever-present!

The fact of His Presence resists my ability to say — so I discard it — not because it doesn't work, for it does work — but because I cannot clothe it in the structure of sentences which is my prelude for proof. The student that I see with the combed hair on his face assumes by that fact the proportions of power to pronounce

This is not for me.

Like the Goddess of reason on the altar of Notre Dame, we deify the less-than-God to avoid the Presence of God Himself. We turn to history which is only a record, or to Science which is a measured prediction, or to Literature which is a reflection of our time, or to Philosophy which raises questions that you cannot answer. We content ourselves with not-knowing when, in point of fact, we do-know, and we underscore the whole situation by our efforts to forget. But what we forget we come to remember. Sooner or later we stand red-faced and alone — waiting and not knowing why — for Christ to say to us

"Come to Me, Child."

Does it disturb your quiet to talk about Christ? It is easier not to talk about Him. Without Him, Good and Evil can be philosophized about — Logic can be construed as the end-all of any discussion. Then Faith becomes horizontal, extending just to *this* man or *this* period or *this* event. Without Christ, there need be no questions about salvation. All of these can be set aside and fashioned into "stories." The whole approach up-lifts us with the intensity and the duration of an aspirin or a martini.

But, whether we like it or not, Christ is an event in the present time. He is ever here to admonish, to warn, and to save. Civil rights and social justice — freedom and morals — the human conscience itself has in some strange way been moved by that string of

"Blessed are's" — or what we call

"The Beatitudes."

It is, and always will be, a question of "Who is the Person?" Rank and authority, — wealth and endowment, — fade and pale as insignificant, when we, like Pilate, are told

"You would have nothing of all this were it not
given to you from above."
I am sanctified by my willing it. For in willing to be sanctified, I have
recognized my place in the universe of time and space. I have the compassion of
those lost with me; those who are the reason for Christ's coming:
"To save that which was lost."

Faith comes easy to those who are enslaved; generosity comes easy to the rich;
pardon comes easy to the powerful. The blood in our streets is such a witness to
this. The blood on Calvary contradicts it all, if, indeed, the word "contradict" is
at all correct. For Christ, the poor must be generous; the rich must believe;
those who are condemned must pardon. If this is a logic, it is the only logic that
makes sense here. When we see that it works, — as work it must — we echo
words long since spoken:
"Truly this *is* God's Son."
"How can we talk about Him?" we say. How can we speak of the past as
though it were here and now a fact? If something has happened, if it is past,
how could it possibly be present here and now? In the ambit of language, and,
with the experience that we accumulate, we are sure that the past *is* the past. It
is such a simple case.
But consider!
God is not in the ambit of language. The language of the wisdom of His words is
geared to this one fact — that God does not act according to tenses.
He just *is*!

Christ knew the problem; He stood up before the learned and the unlearned of
His day to assert simply
"Before Abraham was real, I am."
The gasp of the crowd was lost in the sequential pattern that followed in His
life. So many years later, it would be written that
"He was the Word and the Word was God."

When we see the inner meaning of the events that prompt our words, then
we shall see that the event is prior to the word it prompts. The fact of His

presence is the string of our conscience; the realization of right and wrong; the shame of the nakedness of truth. Adam was ashamed, not because it is a shame to be naked, but because nakedness had no such connotation before. Christ still speaks in the present tense for He is present to us. History is a human problem. To make it more is to endow it with an importance it cannot handle. The fact of God is the fact here and now

of His be-ing.

Words are like wine sacks; once used, they are useless. The new wine needs new sacks. God gave man knees to fall upon — to assume the position of

"be-ing under."

To look back and to look ahead are in the experience of men. To be — to be here and now — is the Fact of God. Christ stands out as the Light of the world; we walk in darkness, for our eyes are hidden and we do not see. But in all and through all the fact remains —

"the light shines in the darkness and the darkness does not grasp it." This is the fact

"of His be-ing."

The world and all it contains — its Full-ness — Open-ness — evil-ness

are mine!

This has been told to me.

And this is a deception!

Not merely deceiving —

But such a deception!

Am I a black or a white,

Am I yellow or a red,

Am I a Jew or a Moslem,

Am I a Catholic or a Protestant —

Or even a Christian?

Where do I live; where do I toil and labor! Where are my roots?

Do not these factors determine what I own — or *can* own —

or even, God forbid,

What I am!

What in the world did Christ come for?

The answer lies not in world history but it lies in myself, as I put the question to myself. It lies in every untruth — every fabrication ever made — every politician's prepared diatribe — every false priest's "holy" echo. The truth lies here in me and here only; we want so to see it. The whitened sepulchres of the scorn of Christ are

Men!

Who are such men? They are the "holy" men — the "wise" men — the "busy" men — the "indolent" of spirit. They are the preachers — the leaders — the pastors of souls whose hands are too filled to hold a soul — whose eyes are too blighted to see the dullness of the streets on which they walk. Were there a mirror here — God forbid — though I deny it, I would see

Myself!

His words of forgiveness were so forceful; yet how could this be? Christ was in the beginning of an agony — the start of human defeat for He was about to die. And yet the cry went out — not from a *conquered* hero but from one who *was conquering:*

"Father forgive them for they know not what they do."

Two thousand years have passed and still we are at a loss for what to do. The structure of our society seems to hem us in, and we are trapped in a world of authoritative compartments. Ask yourself, "How can this be?" Is it not always the case that, "One is your Master, the Christ?"

So many rungs stand out sharply

On Ambition's ladder!

We erect the ladder and therefore it must lead upwards

Or so we think.

Nevertheless to put the question, "What does 'up' mean?" will be the conclusion that of itself 'up' does *not* mean. "Up" is incomprehensible without "down." The ladder of salvation cannot go up! To look even a little closer is to see that salvation has

No ladder!

Union with Christ is not "climbed to"; it is achieved here in the consciousness of "being-with-Christ." So it is that we must be forgiven, for we too

"do not know."

Whether or not this is an indictment, I do not know. However, even Christ chided Thomas for not knowing. He did not chide him because he did not know, but, rather, because he should have known.

> "Have I been with you for so long a time, Thomas, and you do not know."

We hear so much about freedom — about "freedom to" instead of "freedom from" — but this is not the freedom of the Sons of God. That freedom is both "from" and "to." This was the mission of Christ, "to make men free." This most assuredly was a

Freedom from!

To be free from darkness and the powers that bind us to the world in which we live — this is the freedom of Christ. The logical distinctions that spring from the separation of "from" and "for" are man-made. If they help, perhaps they are good; if they confuse, then

Ignore them.

The Analysts are so helpful here, not because they have answers to questions that we ask; not because they analyze meanings to achieve the clarity that makes moral action reasonable; but rather because

> They sharpen the limits of the questions!

Am I free?

> Were the question so easily put and so quickly answered; were the meaning so easily seen in the "freedom for" and "freedom from" discussion; then should Christ have made so much a point out of setting us free? Christ who never explained mystery — who confused and then sought no escape from the confusion — who offered His Body and Blood as *the* Lamb of Sacrifice — This Christ said He would make men free. He who is made free has not

been free before! All this was a freedom from Sin, for He had come
"To give my life as a Ransom for the many."
In how many memories do the fashioners of freedom parade by me now!
In the structure of the established Church with
emphasis on what *must* be done;
In the academic situation of the analysis
of the moral "ought";
In the countless books
that should never have been written;
In the infinity of words
that should never have been spoken.
The fact was already established; We are free because
Christ died!
This is the freedom directed toward living, as He said "in the fullness of life" —
The freedom of "the children of God"

Authority, Christ said to Pilate, comes from above and it is a "given",
Freedom comes from the loosed bond of darkness
and sin, and it is not a "given" —
It is a human fact.
Light and Darkness, Slave and Free, "Thou shalt not" and "Please come to
Me," God and Man, Father and Son; the whole cast of this genuine drama
blend together so that we are free. The death on the cross and its preface,
"Father forgive them," are the shaping
of Freedom.
Take your gift as you take your manhood! The fact is not debatable! It is
Yours!

To be free is to be a person in the fullest sense of that meaning. It means to walk
with your head held high and with a steady step. The gift that Christ offers and
the trust whereby we accept that gift are from Christ too. Whatever denies such
personal stature whether in government, or family or religious community is at
odds with Christ. Though "authority," in this sense, be Christian in label, it is
opposed to Christ. We cannot condone it, even though we pray the prayer of

Christ — "Forgive them, they do not understand" but
    they should have understood!

The history of the world notwithstanding,
    The tragedy of living all too deeply underscored,
        The price of individual peace,
            A mind at rest ...
All these are the testament to Christian Infidelity! In the name of Christ men
have been hounded — wars have been fought — torture has been condoned —
people have been enslaved. And for what?
    To enrich and to powerfy,
        To glorify a family name,
            To win a place in history,
                To preserve that which should never have been founded —
                    A prison!
It is a sin to exploit a sin;
    There is a guilt to imposing guilt;
        It is an abomination to sit in splendor and
                  Pontificate.
When a Church is just a building,
    When worship is just a lecture,
        When liturgy is just a concert,
                Men have gone mad!
If I say to you,
    "You must offer this up," and I do otherwise; "I am a Sinner," and
    condemn your approbation; "I speak for God," when I do not...
Christ has died in vain for me!
      I cannot sit in luxury and claim to be a
    Christian. I cannot associate with the "rich" because they are rich and call
    the "poor" my brothers. I cannot look down on the masses with contempt,
    when in reality, I, too, am part of the masses. I cannot condemn the agnostic
    when I do not believe myself. This is the greatest of all delusions because it
    is not really a delusion. It is really more!
                A Deceit.

The legalism that Christ condemned has been re-erected
　　in the name of Christ.
The world of misery which Christ loved has been em-
　　prisoned in the name of Christ
The sinner whom Christ forgave has been condemned
　　in the name of Christ.
Perhaps His words have a clarity *now* that they never had before:
　　"The time will come when they shall kill you and deem it a service to God."

Christ wept over Jerusalem
　　Though He would die outside its walls.
Christ raised the brother of Martha to life
　　though He promised us Eternal Life.
How much of the "paradox" lies in "mystery?"
　　For this reason we do not seek "understanding"
　　　　We pray for "Faith."
Mystery becomes an absurdity when it is analyzed;
　　Religion becomes a "logic" when it is proved;
　　　　God becomes a "nothing" when we talk about Him so
　　　　　　　　　　　　rhetorically
　　And then believe our foolish words.
　　The answers of the "learned" are always vague enough to be acceptable.
　　Though the question be particular, the answer is always general. For this
　reason, in the precision of language, such are not, nor ever could be,
　　　　　　　　　Answers!
If we could only see that there are no answers in the sense in which we use the
word! The question, "Why?" put to the Acts of God demands a knowledge of
His motive; and this is not just a motive, but the motive of God. However:

　　"Who has ever known the mind of God or who has been His Advisor?"
The answer to all questions is the embodied Christ. His answers raise more
questions than they resolve. "I am the living bread" — "I am the vine" — "I
am the Truth" and the whole litany of His words tear out the compactness of
our syllogisms and rip asunder the fabric of our inference patterns. "Father,

forgive them," He said in prayer. Once that is said I must pray it too: —
"Father, forgive me."

The poet, the logician or even the magician need a word for the precision it guarantees. Christ uses His words for the excitation they arouse in the depths of those who *listen* to Him.

Let me love the "Mystery" not because I understand it — because I do not understand it; let me love the "Mystery" because it binds me to Him who *is* the Mystery. But here the Mystery is the "key." If I accept the Mystery, though it does not make "reasonable" sense, the world *does* then make reasonable sense, and my life, and my aspirations, and my struggle.

This is at once the meaning of the Christian Message: it makes everything else meaningful. I have not seen this meaning and so I am in anguish. I pray, "Father, forgive me," and there is no mystery to that.

Though I sin,
Though I fall,
Though I do not understand,
Still I believe!
"Lord to whom shall I go — You have the words of Eternal Life"
Christ!
It is to You and to You alone that
I go!

VII.
THE BETTER PART

There can be such a peace in words.

These are not the "talked" words which are merely sounded with the proficiency of an instrument. When we talk words, they do not have to make senseful dialogue, nor do they have to convey anything except the fact of speech. In such a way a singer mouths a foreign song — making the proper sounds, but missing for himself the meaning of the lyrics. Even the parrot can "talk" like this.

True words are "spoken" and so they communicate:

The warmth of a person,

His attitudes and personality,

His feelings and his conscious content.

There can be peace spoken in words like these.

Sometimes the recognition of peace is hard to come by. This is not because words are mis-understood, but because the speaker is never heard precisely as he speaks. This is the difficulty most common to the Christian who does not "listen" when Christ speaks to him. We have become so accustomed to "talking" that we fail to see that Christ "speaks." Did He not cry out:

"He who has ears to hear

let him hear."

The plain truth is that

The Christian has lost contact with

CHRIST.

Christ is not merely *in* history, or *in* the past. The whole point of my belief is that I am convinced of His constant PRESENCE. Contact can only be made in the present and

        Christ must be so encountered.
When the Christian confronts Christ,
    There is then no problem.
      The real problem is to make this
         Confrontation.
If Christ is living, then I must meet Him
        FACE TO FACE.

If the Christian life is sad, it is also a lonely life. In a certain sense, more than anyone else in the whole world, the Christian is alone. Kierkegaard so well said of man that the fear of being-alone is a sickness unto death. It is only in the refreshing presence of the Almighty that the healing balm of peace dispels this sickness.

In the Presence of Christ
    The Christian life is

        A rapture.
Perhaps this seems strange to us in the cold world of faction and division. Still the peace of Christ is the one advantage we can claim with impunity. This is more than just a promise; it is the solemn testament of Christ. He said,

        "My peace I leave with you."
        This is His testament.

The difficulty with Peace, as willed to us, lies
    Not with Christ Who willed it
      But with us
        To whom it is willed.
The revelation of Christ is a self-revelation that goes on and on without interruption. Christ Who is being-revealed must be seen; and, as seen, He must be confronted.
    The Gospel is the story of
      CHRISTIAN CONFRONTATION.

The end result of the bond that confrontation imposes raises still another question; one perhaps more subtle and, hence, more sophisticated than the first. The question is so simply put:

What is peace?

Such a question, however, to be answerable at all, makes a basic presupposition, which the thinker must disallow. It presupposes that "Peace" is a tangible "something," which it most definitely is not. The Christian does not have a definition of "Peace." Peace is personal and definitions are universal. There is nothing to compare the personal with; it is unique. Such is the peace of Christ.
The peace of Christ is different.
It must be experienced personally
Like a pain or a joy.
Peace permits recognition through the sensed words of language which communicate our feelings as persons but which cannot define them. Peace cannot be defined.
It can only be felt and welcomed within
the deepest realms of our own experience.
Such is the HERITAGE of Christ.

We do not seek after peace as we seek after other things. If we live our life as Christ admonishes, then the peace itself is intimately realized; it is just there. It is like a Gospel inspiration — we just discover it within ourselves.

Every message is a connected sequence of meanings.
The Message of Christ is no exception but here
the Meanings are uniquely proper to the Message.
Such meanings are found no where else. They have a simplicity and a complexity such that they cannot be exhausted by any one seeker. We examine them; we accept them; we know and re-know them in a cease-less effort to build up our lives. The reflections of others help us to see them more clearly; but, in the final analysis, each person
must see for HIMSELF.

Just as the Christian life must be my life
    Just so the Christian Message is addressed just to me.
        It must be known personally
            JUST BY ME.

The proposition of Christian living is an existential one. It engages the whole person. The uniqueness of the person is the underlying theme of the Message of Christ. The dignity of the individual as a child is the heritage of God. The Christian is the bearer of Christ; so he stands, in faithful imitation of his Master, and cries to heaven. The plan of Redemption is centered in him, and precisely

            As a PERSON.
The Christian faces God Himself
    In the sublime majesty of His awesome power.
The Christian, like Christ, calls God a Father
    And so He is a SON.

The thoughts that I think must be the thoughts of Christ translated into the language peculiar to me. This is an individual language. It is a dialogue with Christ, and it is a continuous one. It is constant and living; person-to-person and face-to-face. It runs back and forth; not just out. These are my words which spring from me and then return enriched by the presence of the "Other," who is Christ. It is in this sense that Faith is

            A LEAP.

It bridges the irrational
    It spans interpersonal space
        It gives the true basis for knowing
            CHRIST.

Christ is the "light of the world" Who will not let us
            Walk in darkness.
The world has never been less than a world of turmoil. There have always been conflagration and distress, only the instruments that cause them have increased

in diabolical quality. There has always been the precarious balance between power and the lack of power — between good and evil — between the differences of racial strain and geographical color and belief. Notwithstanding all these elements, disorder is always discovered most closely between
Man and Man.
The precious shade that divides right and wrong.
The partisan commemorations of victory

The cry of oppression. This is the "master plan" of
The Absurd!
The language of revolution is not always good nor always
Evil!
It all depends. Herein lies the possibility of
Human Choice.

Sentiments beautifully voiced are in literature and the recreation of the situation of living is the task of drama. These are secondhand involvements which derive their meaning and clarity, not from the expression of what is told, but from the reflection of the story with
lived lives.
There is such a temptation in living to make language do more and be more than could possibly be expected from it. We talk so much about Man-kind and Choice and Law and Common Good that in the end we make all these expressions to be more than words; they seem to become, for good or bad, the
Reality!
But truly there is
No "Mankind,"
No "Law,"
No "COMMON Good,"
No "Choice."

There are only:
This and that person,
This and that happy situation,

This and that individual who lives and
Chooses!

We speak of pain and poverty and want! Forgetting that these are abstractions;
forgetting that the reality is the person here and now living in his own solitude
— not part of a conglomeration but an identity here and now
being realized!
Christ said it so well when he demanded: "Is the Sabbath for man or is man for
the Sabbath?" He did not take the position of just "being against sin," but He
came to save Sinners. He did not redeem mankind but He gave His life for the
individuals who compose
The Many.
The logic of Systems works well on the written page; it does not work so well in
my daily life. God forbid! If it did I would be
Less-than-a-man.

The blood in our streets or on our battlefields does not come from the mere
abstraction. Abstractions do not bleed, only men do! Black Power or White
Power; Freedom or Slavery; or any other label is just that!
A Label.
Of all people, the Christian should see this so clearly. To underscore it God
became Man so that we could live, and die if necessary, for what is Personal.
Perhaps this is what has been so wrong! As though *Christianity* or the *Church*
or the *Faith* were the
"Thing"
And not Christ!
We could wage wars for Christianity
but never for Christ!
For Him we turn the other cheek and say,
"Father forgive them."
This Message is personal — it is individual — it is single — It is not a
"System!"
The person is always disenchanted — not with the System as such, for it is a
logically neat expression of integrating factors — he is disenchanted when he

discovers that the orderly System includes him too! It is perfectly all right to be called — American, or Black or White, or industrious or poor, or what have you. It is wrong — completely wrong — to make the designating label to be the reality which it merely designates. The reality is

The Person!

Language labels are always vague enough to be acceptable to others. It is when we are molded into place in a vast logic that has no basis except in speech that we

Recoil!

If the minister of Christ does not see this, who will see it ever? It is then that we join hands in the never ending procession that leads

Nowhere!

For this reason it was said:

"When the blind lead the blind
both fall into the Pit."

In a wide sense, if I am blind, then I am unaware of what it means to be sighted. Thus the affliction that I suffer is predicated of all men, for I know of nothing else.

When I begin to see, the affliction of blindness is then the cause. For how long have we all been blind!

To see again that men are men,
To clarify the vision of human-ness,
To dwell on the light of clearly perceiving

That groups as groups are so unimportant. Not because they are groups because groups are collections of individuals — but rather because the group has supplanted the individual. To be anything at all — one must first be

A Man.

If I choose of myself, the choice is something. If the choosing is not mine but that of the group, then I have not chosen at all. The pattern is never clear of itself, but against the background of human activity, it all stands out so boldly. The activity of "doing" because that is the fashion; of "serving" because that is the accepted plan; of "obeying" because we have no choice! This is the picture of

82

life. However, in the midst of all those who so acted; in the face of the facts designated by society as "proper," Christ answered the rebuke of Martha and looked at Mary with Godly love. His answer was so well said: Be not upset about her for she has chosen

"The Better Part."

It is this that I must try to see and understand! That there is a "better part" and that it can be chosen

by Me!

The better part is to welcome the values of living as real, letting them begin to exercise their moral worth in my life. It is to see every man precisely as a person — for in so seeing him there is

No color that blinds me,

No belief that repels me.

No sin for which I am not sorry,

No blessing that I would not give.

We walk to Calvary everyday anyway. To be sure that it is the Calvary of Christ is the only way to insure

Peace!

If I could break out of the Group

There would be no establishment!

If my life were a demonstration

I would be my own banner!

If I could properly locate learning

There would be room for Faith

If I could see God as I should

Proof would be worthless

And it is!

If I could learn to love, I would know God.

He is Love.

The *simplicity* of life is a startling discovery. It disturbs me to see it so! It is easier to see life's *complexity* for this serves to excuse me. If life is complex, if complicated, if forbidding, then my living it is pre-judged in that light. Perhaps, after all these years, that was the real purpose of Christ, to underscore simplicity. Perhaps for this reason, He asked for

    The trust of the child.

        The love of the child.

           The response of the child.

Perhaps too, this is why everything is so simple — and also why the answer to life is so simple. This is the answer:

    "You must love God first

        And then your brother."

My brother is every other man. To love like this is indeed a choice. It is

           The Better Part!

EPILOGUE

Language is not natural such that it has always been there, just to use and enjoy. Language is a human construct, wherein, given a certain culture (due mainly though not exclusively to some accidental setting), sounds are vocalized to signify meanings which are spoken syntactically and grammatically in a definite form. This fact colors our world and makes it appear as we speak it. We voice sounds and they become the labels for the world of discourse. Right or wrong or otherwise, we communicate in that way. Labels are just attached to things. So, the sun "sets" and "rises," there is an "up" and a "down," and persons are solid things to be encountered, loved and dealt with. But this world of language is not the *only* world. There are worlds that are extra-lingual; the world of all living things, as well as the world of children. There is a language here too and a logic that the grown-up does not know, nor could he. Here is the story of one child who, through the magic of "our" words, will describe his universe and his life. We may call it a fantasy; but then what is real anyway?

My name is David. How old I am does not matter because I belong to a whole company of little people who are banded together precisely because of "being-little." The number of years that I have accumulated is unimportant; but the number of years that you have lived is not. If you do not understand, then you belong to a different group, thoroughly disorganized and often at odds, which is the world of the *Grown-Up-Adult*. We call you simply a *"GUA."* You may not understand us, but we understand you. You believe that you are very complex and sophisticated, but, truly, are you? You are really like an uncomplicated number. You are a "One," or a "Two." Something just there; uncomplicated though so complicating.

My name is David because you gave it to me. You assigned a sound to a little bundle of nerves and energy. You write the name down on a certificate and I have to answer to it for the rest of my life.

Later on, perhaps, when I become a *GUA*, it will mean something to me; perhaps I shall be glad for it, for then, at that time, I too will have left this name-less paradise. Perhaps, then, I too shall have traded the complexity of this beauty for the simplicity of the dull life; I will have become a regimented *GUA* and my memory will have become clouded, and I will have forgotten what life really is. I, too, I guess, will have to trade the reality of this wonderfully full existence for the fantasy of adulthood. That very idea makes me sad.

I want to begin with something that is so familiar to us all — even to *GUA's*. Do you know that tree in the yard? It sings when the wind brushes the branches. It has a melody and a message, which are part of my world and so you cannot understand them. These sounds have no place in your world of discourse, and, so, you laugh at them as though they were incoherent.

Let me try to tell you what the songs say. The gentle songs tell of God, and the beauty of the sky; they tell of angels, all of which I can see so plainly. They come out of their world and show themselves; but only to those who can see them. They are make-believe to you, but, do you know, *you* are just make-believe to them? You and they are worlds apart; it is only we, in the complexity of our childhood, who can take the short step out of one world into the other.

Dear *GUA's,* the universe is so much larger than your language patterns permit you to imagine. I am afraid of your world, but if mine is mysterious, it is very beautiful. I dread the time when I too must "forget" and come to live in the narrow world of things, and words and speech. I cease to be a child, when the name "David" is my label of adulthood, I shall have forgotten.

There are so many things I have to talk about. I would like to describe my world in its totality, but that is impossible, for the totality is far too complex to be so briefly described. Here there is no "right" and "wrong" in the legal sense.

There are no laws enacted to distribute justice, for here we don't have a meaning for justice. It is only a question of each one doing what he is supposed to do. The dog barks, the bird sings, the sun shines, the clouds rain, the flowers grow, and we live. Even the evil here is beautiful. You might call it sickness or disease; here we call it "ending" in a way decreed by the structure of our world.

Life is no mystery here, for everything lives in one way or another. We don't have a meaning for death, for to be is to live, and to communicate, and to develop. This sounds contradictory to you, for it does not fit into your logic, but, if you saw God, as a child does, your logic would be so empty. Even apart from that fact, it is empty anyway. Just think! What is logical about love? about emotions? about feelings? There is only logic in reasoning, and that involves thoughts and concepts. The *GUA* reasons and discovers; but what?

I have traveled to the moon a thousand times. I have seen the stars and blinked at their brightness. I have walked in space, and explored countless passages that could never be mapped out; because here there is no map. Maps are no good except for the spatial and temporal facts that you have mistaken for the whole of what is real. How many times have I looked at you and asked that question, "What is real?" You didn't hear the question much less *answer* it. Do you know why? Only because you think that all questions must be asked in words. Words are only language sounds that some men have made up and other men have studied. But, as such, the Russian cannot talk to the Greek, nor the Jew to the Scot, for their words or sounds aren't the same. It is for much the same reason that you cannot talk to me, except that I have no words at all. Or, if you could only see that words are so small a part of life. You don't love in words, do you?

Sometimes you come so close to seeing what I know to be real. The conviction you cannot "prove"; the knowledge that a friend is true; the affection of a wife that is just there in her heart without your "being told" about it. If only you could become complicated like the world. Nothing is as simple as you think. It's not just this or that; good and bad; white and yellow, red and black. It's a harmony of color, sound, feeling and meaning that could never be expressed in a single thought, much less declared in a sentence. It's a sentiment, and a feeling, and a reaching-out and a touching and loving. Dear *GUA*, it is just "seeing." Some day when I too am a *GUA*, when I look back on the treasures of my childhood, when I see them as you do now, then I too will wonder about the special value they have. But then the memory of the child will have been dimmed, and the beauty and richness of real living will have been lost, and they will just be childish fantasies to me too.

But now I am a child and my world is the real world that surrounds me. I should tell you how vividly I see God. I wish I could explain what that means, but I cannot in your words; and that is all that you understand. God is not up in the sky, high up in the clouds. God is right here with me. I don't pray to God; I talk to him. He is not a man or a woman; or a thing; or a toy. Nothing like that at all! He is a beautiful vision so near to me that I am drawn to Him. He fills my whole world, and I am very important in that world. I feel His finger on my shoulder, and on my heart. I talk to Him without sounds, but with so much meaning. From Him I know that love is not a word, but a doing; an embracing. It is you I worry about, for you have missed the sight of Him. Yet, of all the things in my world, this alone is the one sight you should never miss.

Sophistication makes for such shallowness. To be learned is to know how much we do not know. Language is a tool for some types of communication; it is not the map of the universe. The question, "What is really real?" is a tantalizing one. When you see a little child again, ask yourself that question and you may be surprised at the answer you get. How wonderful it would be to be a little David once more and see so clearly that beauty is very complex, and very filling and all engulfing.

A CONCLUDING POSTSCRIPT

Every beginning involves something of a conclusion, and, in our everyday experience, every conclusion distinctly reflects its own beginning. In the Christian sense, beginning and ending are terms of a remarkably definite kind. For us, the beginning is just the start. It is simply the commencement of "living," and that living shall be finally engulfed in an overwhelming conclusion. "Life" and "Death," on the other hand, are just language words which reflect insufficiently the contents of the Revealed Message. For the Christian, "Death" is not a conclusion in *just* the language sense. In its deepest sense, "Death" does not conclude; it merely points again to another beginning. This is a uniquely closed cycle which cannot be verified by human experience nor in any way tested by scientific perception. The communicated fact is just believed, but that belief is centered in the strongest certitude possible, the conviction which comes from Christ revealing. It is Christ saying, "I am the Way and the Life." To live in Christ means to live always, and, although Death is a change, it is *just* a change, not an ending. Christ is life, and He is life in a much more meaningful manner than the "language-sense" declares.

The conscious act either of direct encounter, or intuition, or faith is most basically the-aware-ness-of-something. Briefly, there are, upon analysis, three "irreducibles" involved here. They are all intermingled in the knowing activity, but they are, none the less, distinct and distinguishable. I refer to the state-of-mind of the knower; his personal awareness; and the evidence or basis which makes that awareness acceptable to him, such that he affirms or denies that of which he is aware. In the conscious activity of "Christian Belief," the state-of-mind of the believer is characterized by a certitude which is not conditioned by any attitude less than that. In this instance, the evidential support is nothing more or less than what the Christian believes; namely, God-speaking-through-Christ. The believer gives his total assent to these words without question, for the Christian is a spiritual "child." It is this trust in Christ that distinguishes Him as an individual in the world, and which gives Him a unique pattern for living.

The Christian must learn to communicate with Christ. He does this through prayer. However, we should make some concluding remarks here. When we think about communication in the ordinary human sense, we immediately think of language. Nevertheless, though language is a *kind* of communication, it is certainly not the only kind. The love of person for person, to cite an instance, exceeds the limits of language. When love is communicated, the words expressed are not adequate, but the meaning is achieved, because it is "felt" in a uniquely personal way. It is not "sensed" like seeing, or hearing, or touching; but it *is* "sensed" in some strange manner that is, at rock bottom, the involvement of the total person, as knowing and feeling and emoting. Presence is communicated in this way too. For this reason the presence of Christ must be felt as "person-feels-person," and Christ be loved as "person-loves-person." There is no dimensional space between Christ and the Christian. He is "there" and, if I believe, I must be open to him precisely as "there."

"Christian Believing" and "Christian Love" and "Christian Feeling" are new strata of conscious achievement. God is the Unspeakable, but Christ is His spoken Word. Once God speaks this Word, as He did at the Incarnation, and it is taught to us, then we can speak it too. This we try to do even in the face of the incomprehensible and the mysterious, as when we believe as the Christian must believe. Perhaps the following aphorism will bring out our point:

> In one classroom a Scholastic Professor concluded his lecture and then announced, "I have 'proved' beyond a doubt that God is real." His students nodded in agreement.

> In another classroom, an Atheist concluded his lecture and he an-

nounced, ''I have just 'proved' that God does not exist.'' His students nodded in agreement.

In still another classroom an Agnostic concluded his lecture and he announced, ''I have just 'proved' that we can never be sure whether there is a God or there is not a God.'' His students nodded in agreement.

God looked in on all three classrooms
and just smiled.